Ayurveda

& energy healing

Ayurveda
& energy healing

Using earth energies, crystals and colour for health and vitality

SALLY MORNINGSTAR
LILIAN VERNER-BONDS
SIMON LILLY

LORENZ BOOKS

This edition is published by Lorenz Books

Lorenz Books is an imprint of Anness Publishing Ltd
Hermes House, 88–89 Blackfriars Road, London SE1 8HA
tel. 020 7401 2077; fax 020 7633 9499
www.southwaterbooks.com; info@anness.com

© Anness Publishing Ltd 2004

UK agent: The Manning Partnership Ltd
6 The Old Dairy, Melcombe Road, Bath BA2 3LR
tel. 01225 478444; fax 01225 478440; sales@manning-partnership.co.uk

UK distributor: Grantham Book Services Ltd
Isaac Newton Way, Alma Park Industrial Estate, Grantham, Lincs NG31 9SD
tel. 01476 541080; fax 01476 541061; orders@gbs.tbs-ltd.co.uk

North American agent/distributor: National Book Network
4501 Forbes Boulevard, Suite 200, Lanham, MD 20706
tel. 301 459 3366; fax 301 429 5746; www.nbnbooks.com

Australian agent/distributor: Pan Macmillan Australia
Level 18, St Martins Tower, 31 Market St, Sydney, NSW 2000
tel. 1300 135 113; fax 1300 135 103; customer.service@macmillan.com.au

New Zealand agent/distributor: David Bateman Ltd
30 Tarndale Grove, Off Bush Road, Albany, Auckland
tel. (09) 415 7664; fax (09) 415 8892

A CIP catalogue record for this book is available from the British Library.

Publisher: Joanna Lorenz
Editorial Director: Helen Sudell
Project Editors: Sarah Duffin, Fiona Eaton
Designers: Allan Mole, Nigel Partridge
Photographer: Don Last
Illustrators: Anna Koska, Giovanni Pierce
Production Controller: Darren Price

Previously published in three separate volumes,
Crystals and Crystal Healing, *Colour* and *Ayurveda*

1 3 5 7 9 10 8 6 4 2

PUBLISHER'S NOTE
The reader should not regard the recommendations, ideas and techniques expressed
and described in this book as substitutes for the advice of a qualified medical
practitioner or other qualified professional. Any use to which the recommendations,
ideas and techniques are put is at the reader's sole discretion and risk.

Contents

INTRODUCTION

Here are techniques and exercises to help you to explore and understand the power of three natural therapies to work in harmony together. Why these therapies have such a profound effect is not fully understood but they have been shown to bring about significant improvements in certain conditions. They can affect us physically, emotionally and spiritually by harnessing the subtle energy systems that exist in us all.

Ayurveda is an ancient Indian healing system, which according to your body type offers advice on diet, soothing therapies and exercise routines to work towards harmony of body and spirit.

Colour healing explores the vital influence of colour on our lives and how to use methods such as visualization and meditation to release its healing power and energy.

Crystal healing introduces safe and easy techniques to show how the placement of gemstones can enable you to feel calm, energized and revitalized.

Discover how to benefit from the gentle healing power of ayurveda, colour and crystal therapies, and how to achieve inner peace and physical health.

AYURVEDA
HEALING

Ayurveda is an ancient Indian healing system that has been used for centuries to promote healing and longevity. The many branches of Ayurveda offer a holistic approach to living, encouraging balance and moderation in all things. By assessing the personality, a programme of diet and exercise can be devised to suit each individual that will promote good health and well-being.

THE PRINCIPLES OF AYURVEDA

AYURVEDA IS ACKNOWLEDGED AS THE traditional healing system of India, covering all aspects of life and lifestyle. Thousands of years old, it has influenced many other healing systems around the world. It was already established before the births of Buddha and Christ, and some biblical stories reflect the wisdom of Ayurvedic teachings.

There are many different branches to Ayurveda because it covers so many aspects of health and healing. These have been touched upon in this guide but the main emphasis is on dietary and lifestyle advice, specifically tailored to living in the Western world.

Ayurvedic medicine is founded on the belief that all diseases stem from the digestive system and are caused either by poor digestion of food, which is the body's major source of nourishment, or by following an improper diet for your *dosha* (nature). The system therefore concentrates to a large extent upon nutrition. There are three main humours (characteristics) or doshas – *vata* (ether and wind), *pitta* (fire and water) and *kapha* (water and earth) – and in this book you will find basic advice about suitable

diets for the different doshas, as well as information about supportive treatments, including massage, exercise, colour, crystals, herbs and spices. There is also a tonic drink for each doshic type, and a list of common ailments that can be treated very effectively.

The following basic Ayurvedic approach will help you to develop some simple ways to keep yourself balanced in these days of increasing pressure, worry and stress. Identify your dosha, learn how to eat and live in accordance with your true nature, and discover how you can begin to heal your *vikruti* (current emotional, physical or mental health conditions) with the use of certain basic Ayurvedic methods.

Dosha means "that which tends to go out of balance easily". The elements, the seasons, your astrological chart, your genetic inheritance from your parents and environmental factors: all of these contribute to the potential for imbalance within the doshas. Ayurveda's philosophy is to live in truth – to live in understanding.

Right: Herbs and spices play an important part in treating common ailments.

THE ORIGINS OF AYURVEDA

The origins of Ayurveda are uncertain. It is recounted that thousands of years ago, men of wisdom or *rishis* (meaning seers) as they are known in India, were saddened by the suffering of humanity. They knew that ill health and short lives allowed man little time to consider his spirituality and to commune with the divine – with God. In the Himalayan mountains they prayed and meditated together, calling upon God to help them to relieve the plight of man, and God felt moved by compassion to give them the teachings that would enlighten them in the ways of healing illness and alleviating suffering upon the earth.

It is believed that these teachings are the Vedas, although this cannot be proven, due to the lack of historical records. A book called the *Atharva Veda* was one of the first detailed accounts of the system. From this, and perhaps other ancient writings, came the beginnings of Ayurvedic medicine, which has developed, changed and absorbed many

Above: Meditation has the power to calm the mind and opens the spirit to a greater consciousness. Indian sadhus, like the one pictured here, live a simple nomadic life, renouncing worldly goods in order that they may devote themselves to prayer and meditation.

other influences over hundreds of years to become what it is today. Due to the invasions of India, and the subsequent suppression of the original Indian way of life, several ancient texts have been lost or destroyed, but enough have

survived to ensure the continuation of the teachings.

Ayurveda is acknowledged as the traditional healing system of India. It comes from two Sanskrit words: *ayur*, meaning "life" and *veda*, meaning "knowing", and can be interpreted as "science of life". It is the oldest recorded healing system to remain intact and is extremely comprehensive. It has many different branches and has influenced traditional healing systems around the world.

The fundamental principles of Ayurveda are based upon the Indian philosophy called *Samkhya*, meaning "to know the Truth". The principle of Samkhya is that the basis of life is consciousness and that with the awakening of consciousness comes understanding about the way in which the universe works – including health and healing. Samkhya advocates that to live in the light of truth brings great illumination to the heart of man, and Ayurvedic practices are focused upon leading us toward that truth.

12

THE INFLUENCE OF AYURVEDA

For centuries after the end of the Vedic era, Ayurvedic medicine developed into a comprehensive healing system. Its philosophy and techniques spread from India to China, Arabia, Persia and Greece, influencing Middle Eastern, Greek and Chinese healing practices. It is known that Ayurvedic practitioners reached ancient Athens, and it can be noted that the traditional Greek medicine based upon the bodily humours (characteristics), which will be discussed later in the book, is significantly similar to Ayurveda. Greek medicine strongly influenced the subsequent

Left: Acupuncture is sometimes used in treatments and it is likely that the technique originated in India and later spread to China.

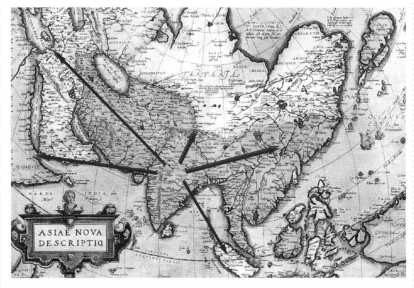

Above: Ayurveda travelled out of India and influenced many other countries with its ageless wisdom about living in the light of truth.

development of traditional Western medicine, but it is difficult to say exactly to what degree the medical philosophy of Ayurveda was influential, or how much Ayurveda influenced Greek and European medicine.

The five elements in Chinese medicine appear to have come from Ayurveda. It is documented that the Indian medical system was brought to China by Indian Buddhist missionaries, many of whom were highly competent

Ayurvedic practitioners. The missionaries also travelled to South-East Asia and Tibet, influencing the people of these lands. Tibetan medicine, for example, is a combination of Ayurvedic practices and philosophy with a Tibetan Buddhist and shamanic influence.

WHAT IS AYURVEDIC MEDICINE?

The main aim of Ayurvedic medicine (which is only one branch of Ayurveda) is to improve health and longevity, leaving the individual free to contemplate matters of the spirit and to follow a spiritual path. This does not mean that you have to be spiritual or religious to benefit from Ayurvedic medicine; the system is very practical in its applications and deals with all kinds of health problems, without spirituality ever being mentioned. Its main

Right: Ayurveda is primarily vegetarian. If meat must be eaten, choose a wild product rather than a commercially reared one, to ensure that the meat is as natural and organic as possible.

focus is nutrition, supported primarily by the use of herbs, massage and aromatic oils, but there are many complementary branches as well.

Ayurvedic philosophy encourages those who practise it to eat the fruits and seeds of the earth, rather than take the life of animals. Some animal products have been included in this introductory guide, but these should be used in moderation.

The branches of Ayurvedic medicine include specific diets, surgery, *jyotish* (Vedic astrology),

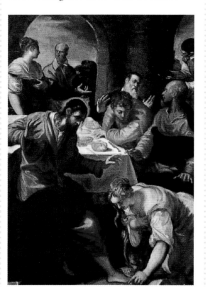

Left: Some of the stories in the bible, such as that in which Mary Magdalene anoints the feet of Christ with oils, are Ayurvedic in nature. It is very likely that this practice stemmed from the Ayurvedic tradition.

psychiatry and *pancha karma* (cleansing and detoxifying techniques). Yoga is not a branch of Ayurveda, but it shares the same roots and so the two are often practised together. Yoga includes meditation, mantras (prayer chants), yantras (contemplation of geometric visual patterns) and hatha yoga (practices for spirit, mind and body harmony). It is yoga that concentrates most precisely upon the more spiritual aspects of the Ayurvedic teachings.

THE BRANCHES OF AYURVEDA

Wherever you go in the world, you will find people working with the elements, with the humours, the seasons and the planets. A humoral type is a mixture of physical, mental or emotional tendencies (influenced by karma in astrology). The physical and mental are not separated but are seen as two sides of the same coin.

In Ayurveda there are hot and cold people, thin and fat people, dry and moist people; these body types will have different tendencies emotionally, mentally and physically, and therefore will be affected by different types of food, herbs and oils.

The very important branch of Ayurvedic medicine called *pancha karma* focuses upon detoxification and uses steam baths, oelation (oiling), enemas and emesis (therapeutic vomiting), plus fasting. This may sound unsavoury to the Western mind, but pancha karma is a very effective way of cleansing the

Left: Certain gems correlate to planets – ruby to the sun and moonstone (as shown left) to the moon for example.

system of toxins, especially those that are stubborn in their release, or have been held in the body for a long time. Pancha karma must only be performed by a qualified practitioner; at the moment it is seriously practised in India, Sri Lanka and the United States, but not yet in the United Kingdom.

Many things influence life on earth. The *jyotish* (Ayurvedic astrologer) assesses the birth chart and the current movement of the planets in the solar system to determine what may affect an

Right: It can sometimes be difficult to set aside the complexities of the material world and spend time in contemplation. Most people benefit from meditation or yoga, which can help to illuminate the pathway to inner peace.

individual's constitution. In order to alleviate potential aggravations from planetary influences, he or she may prescribe gems to wear on certain parts of the body. By following the advice of a jyotish, weak and strong areas of the birth chart can be worked on, to enhance the strengths, and strengthen the weaknessses.

THE DOSHAS AND THE SEASONS

There are three doshas (basic types of people, in terms of constitution) – vata, pitta and kapha. They are influenced by the rhythms of nature, seasonal change and the time of year. Autumn is a time of change when leaves turn brown and dry out; vata is highest in autumn and early winter, and at times of dry, cold and windy weather. Pitta is highest in late spring, throughout the summer and during times of heat and humidity. Kapha is highest in the winter months and

Left: In spring, consider a cleansing fast to clear the body of any excess kapha that may have accumulated during the winter months. When kapha meets pitta in the spring, it can provide the conditions for colds and flu to develop – the body's way of cleansing ama (toxins) and kapha from the system.

Below: Summer, the season of heat and activity, should be tempered with calming colours, soothing scents, and leisurely activities to enhance rest and relaxation.

WARMING UP/SPRING
pitta accumulating, kapha
aggravated, vata neutral

HOT/SUMMER
vata accumulating, pitta
aggravated, kapha decreasing

COOLING/AUTUMN
vata aggravated, pitta
decreasing, kapha neutral

COLD/WINTER
vata decreasing, pitta neutral,
kapha accumulating

Above: Autumn is a time when the weather is changeable, which will increase levels of vata. Ensure that you have some stress-free time in comforting surroundings to help to keep vata in balance, especially if you are a vata dosha or have a vata condition.

during early spring, when the weather is cold and damp.

In Ayurvedic theory, the progress of a disease goes through several stages and this is reflected in seasonal influences upon the doshas. There is the process of accumulation of a dosha (when it is increasing), followed by a time of aggravation (when it is at its highest point and can cause problems). There is a time of decrease (when it is lessening) and a neutral time, when it is passive (neither decreasing nor increasing). These four phases are associated with the seasons, bearing in mind that in different areas climatic conditions or seasonal variations may modify the general principles.

Use the questionnaire later in this book to discover your dosha – vata, pitta or kapha. Single doshic types can simply refer to whichever dosha scores the highest points on their questionnaire. If you discover that you are a dual doshic type, which is quite common, it is generally recommended that you vary your diet and lifestyle to suit the seasonal changes as described in the dual doshas section.

Below: In winter, kapha is accumulating, vata is decreasing and pitta is neutral. Winter is a time when people who live in colder climates tend to want to eat kapha-inducing foods, in other words those that are more fatty and substantial. If you are a kapha dosha or have a kapha condition, try to include plenty of hot spices and warming drinks in your diet.

FINDING YOUR BODY TYPE

This section outlines how you can identify your dosha or body type. Dosha means "that which tends to go out of balance easily". Your dosha is your bio-type or *prakruti* ("nature"). You are made up of a mixture of the five elements of ether, wind, fire, water and earth, and will display certain characteristics, depending upon your basic nature.

As well as your prakruti, you may also have a *vikruti*, which is your current state of mental or physical health. This develops throughout your life and may actually differ from your prakruti. It is important that you treat your vikruti first (how you are now), then go back to living with your prakruti. For example, you may have developed arthritis or back trouble over a long period of time, or you may be suffering from a cold or skin rash which lasts for a few days. Once you have cleared your condition, you can maintain your prakruti by preventative treatment which includes diet, massage, oils, colours and scents as well as an awareness of seasons and planets.

Above: From an Ayurvedic perspective, your astrological birth chart and the predominance of your planets will also give an indication about your disposition.

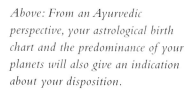

Left: Your dosha is influenced by factors such as environment (workplace, colours, sounds, crystals or habitat), climate, food and drink, as well as other factors such as your emotional state, level of exercise and astrological influences.

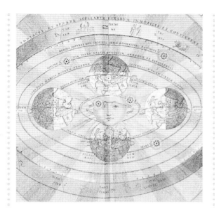

Above: The difference between your prakruti and vikruti can be compared with that between your astrological birth chart and the transits and progressions of the planets. These occur throughout your life and will exert strong influences upon you at certain times, modifying your fixed astrological birth chart as the planets move around the cosmos.

Apart from the three single doshas, there are four combinations, making a total of seven differing constitutional types: vata, pitta, kapha, vata/pitta (or pitta/vata), pitta/kapha (or kapha/pitta), kapha/vata (or vata/kapha), and vata/pitta/kapha. These may be either out of balance or in a state of balance.

To discover your prakruti and vikruti, answer the questionnaire twice. Also ask other people who know you well to fill out the questionnaire for you, to give you as clear a picture of yourself as possible. The first time you fill out the questionnaire, you should concentrate upon your current condition – your vikruti – recording answers based upon the present and your recent health history.

You can discover your prakruti by answering the questionnaire a second time, this time with answers based upon your entire lifetime. Fill out the questionnaire with your complete history in mind. This will give you a better idea about the difference between your vikruti and your prakruti. Once the answers to the questionnaire have revealed both your vikruti and your prakruti (they may be the same, which is fine), the information in this book can be used to treat both. Follow whichever dosha scores most

highly (vata, pitta or kapha), whether you are trying to balance any excess or, having balanced your excess, are trying to maintain a state of balance. You can fill out the questionnaire again at regular intervals to monitor how you are progressing in balancing yourself. If, like many people, you are a dual type, refer to the section on dual doshas for advice on which plan is most suitable for you.

Left: Yoga can be an extremely helpful way to achieve balance of the the body and mind. A large number of the yogic postures are named after things from the natural world, such as animals and trees. This is to help us to connect with these energies and in doing so strengthen our connection to the dance of life in our universe. Yoga can be used as part of an exercise plan to help to balance the doshas very effectively.

ELEMENTAL ENERGIES

The elements are very important in Ayurveda. They descend from space (ether), down to air. Air descends into the fire element. Fire falls into the water element and water to earth, so that we move from the most rarefied of the elements (ether) to the most dense (earth). With this in mind, you will notice that the chart below follows a descending pattern of ether and air (vata), fire and water (pitta) and water and earth (kapha). Vata is a mixture of ether and air and is often translated as "wind". In the creation story of Ayurveda, vata leads the other doshas, because its air-and-ether combination is the most rarefied. The elements move from the most refined down to the most dense. So, if vata is out of balance, this will generally make the others go out of balance as well.

Your age and the season of the year will also have an influence upon your doshic type. From childhood up to the teenage years you are

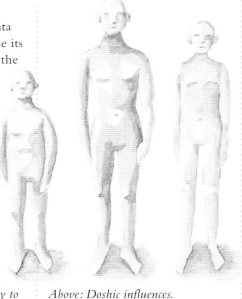

Left: People in the West are likely to have a problem with an excess of vata, in spite of the fact that there may be very little vata in the basic constitution. Vata relates to stress and the nervous system, and also to depletion, so will probably need treating to some extent.

Above: Doshic influences. Left: childhood, susceptibility to kapha conditions, such as colds. Centre: mid-life, risk of pitta conditions, such as digestive problems and headaches. Right: old age, susceptibility to vata conditions, such as arthritis and flatulence.

ELEMENT	DOSHA	COSMIC LINK	PRINCIPLE	INFLUENCE
ether/air	vata	wind	change	activity/movement
fire/water	pitta	sun	conversion	metabolism/transformation
water/earth	kapha	moon	inertia	cohesion

Above: A vata type will be susceptible to excess "wind" or air, and will be potentially changeable, with a fairly active personality.

influenced by kapha; from your teens to the age of 50 or 60 you tend to come under the pitta influence, and from 50 to 60 onwards you enter the vata phase of life.

Each dosha has a particular energetic activity or principle, which influences certain

responses within the body. Everyone has all three doshas to some extent; it is their ratio to each other which is important, and it is this ratio which makes up our individuality. Each dosha plays an important role. For example movement (vata) without the stability of kapha would be chaos, and the inactivity of kapha without activity and movement would result in stagnation. Ayurveda sometimes refers to deficiencies, but usually considers the doshas in excess (too much pitta, for example). An excess of kapha would therefore indicate a need

Below: A pitta type will have the potential for excess fire, like a hot sun, and will be able to transform or change things quite easily.

Above: A kapha type (water and earth) will be intuitive, sensitive and will dislike change but will be good at holding things together.

for a kapha-reducing eating and living plan, and the information in this introductory guide has been geared to deal with excesses in each of the doshas.

You will have an excess if you score significantly higher in one dosha than you do in the other two doshas.

USING THE QUESTIONNAIRE

The questionnaire overleaf is designed to help you to assess your basic ratio of humoral factors. From this you can determine which diet, colours, exercise routines, crystals, oils and scents are most likely to suit you. By referring to the sections on which you score the most points, you will identify whether you are a vata, pitta or kapha dosha, or a combination type. Read the questions and, to discover your prakruti, tick those descriptions which apply to you in general terms. Allocate two ticks to the statement that is most applicable to you; use one tick for a description that could also apply, and if a description does not apply to you, leave it unticked.

As has already been explained, your current condition, or vikruti, may not be the same as your underlying constitution, or prakruti. If you wish to discover whether or not this is the case, go through the questions a second time, this time using crosses instead of ticks. To reveal your vikruti, answer the questions

according to how you have been feeling more recently, and how the descriptions relate to your current health or condition, including any illnesses or other changes you are experiencing.

When you are answering the questions, make sure that you focus either on your prakruti (general state throughout your life – ticks), or on your vikruti

Above: Vatas need to learn how to be still and grounded, because they have the least amount of stamina they are much more likely to suffer from energy depletion.

(current or recent state – crosses). To avoid confusion, finish with one set of answers before you start to fill out and assess the questionnaire a second time.

If you wish, you can answer the questionnaire a third time, separating questions about the mind from questions about the body. Use circles and squares to record your answers. This will give you an idea as to whether your mind and your body are the same dosha or different. If they are different, you can follow the dietary advice for the body and the lifestyle advice for the mind, outlined in the relevant sections on doshas. For example, if you have a kapha body and a pitta mind, you would follow the kapha eating and exercise plan, including the massage technique, and ensure that you have cooling, soothing colours and a calm working and living environment with a certain amount of challenge to keep the pitta mind as balanced as possible.

Following the questionnaire are three sections headed "Vata",

Left: Gems are used in Ayurveda only with a prescription from a jyotish (Vedic or Hindu astrologer) or from an Ayurvedic physician. Set into a ring, they are worn on a specific finger.

Above: A jyotish will consult the planets and your astrological chart before working with crystals. Minerals should be treated with caution in case they are contra-indicated by your birth chart.

Right: Choose herbs carefully, ensuring that they are suitable for your particular doshic condition.

"Pitta" and "Kapha". Having discovered your vikruti (condition) or prakruti (constitution), turn to the pages relevant to your predominant dosha, for detailed advice on reducing any excess (vikruti), or for maintaining your true character (prakruti). When referring to the various sections, please read the information very carefully before you begin to put it into practice.

When using Ayurvedic medicinal herbs, remember to take them only as long as you are experiencing symptoms. Check that the herbs are still suited to your doshic needs on a regular basis.

When you begin to use any of the Ayurvedic prescriptions and techniques, do not be tempted to elaborate on them. Ayurveda is extremely complex and precise. For example, there are guidelines about the specific crystals that may be used to make a crystal infusion for each dosha. It is advisable that you do not make other infusions unless you are qualified or

Left: Choose oils according to your doshic condition.

experienced; crystals and gems can have a very powerful effect, so they must be used with respect and caution. If you find you do not feel good when wearing a particular crystal or gem, then you should remove it.

DISCOVER YOUR DOSHA
Mark the questionnaire with either a √ (= your general constitution – prakruti) or x (= your current or recent state – vikruti).

	VATA	PITTA	KAPHA
HEIGHT	Very short, or tall and thin	Medium	Tall or short and sturdy
MUSCULATURE	Thin, prominent tendons	Medium/firm	Plentiful/solid
BODILY FRAME	Light, narrow	Medium frame	Large/broad
WEIGHT	Light, hard to gain	Medium weight	Heavy, gains easily
SWEAT	Minimal	Profuse, especially when hot	Moderate
SKIN	Dry, cold	Soft, warm	Moist, cool, possibly oily
COMPLEXION	Darkish	Fair, pink, red, freckles	Pale, white
HAIR AMOUNT	Average amount	Early thinning and greying	Plentiful
TYPE OF HAIR	Dry, thin, dark, coarse	Fine, soft, red, fair	Thick, lustrous, brown
SIZE OF EYES	Small, narrow or sunken	Average	Large, prominent
TYPE OF EYES	Dark brown or grey, dull	Blue/grey/hazel, intense	Blue, brown, attractive
TEETH AND GUMS	Protruding, receding gums	Yellowish, gums bleed	White teeth, strong gums
SIZE OF TEETH	Small or large, irregular	Average	Large
PHYSICAL ACTIVITY	Moves quickly, active	Moderate pace, average	Slow pace, steady
ENDURANCE	Low	Good	Very good
STRENGTH	Poor	Good	Very good
TEMPERATURE	Dislikes cold, likes warmth	Likes coolness	Aversion to cool and damp
STOOLS	Tendency to constipation	Tendency to loose stools	Plentiful, slow elimination
LIFESTYLE	Variable, erratic	Busy, tends to achieve a lot	Steady, can skip meals
SLEEP	Light, interrupted, fitful	Sound, short	Deep, likes plenty
EMOTIONAL TENDENCY	Fearful, anxious, insecure	Fiery, angry, judgmental	Greedy, possessive
MENTAL ACTIVITY	Restless, lots of ideas	Sharp, precise, logical	Calm, steady, stable
MEMORY	Good recent memory	Sharp, generally good	Good long term
REACTION TO STRESS	Excites very easily	Quick temper	Not easily irritated
WORK	Creative	Intellectual	Caring
MOODS	Change quickly	Change slowly	Generally steady
SPEECH	Fast	Clear, sharp, precise	Deep, slow
RESTING PULSE			
WOMEN	Above 80	70-80	Below 70
MEN	Above 70	60-70	Below 60
Totals: *Please add up*	**Vata**	**Pitta**	**Kapha**

AYURVEDIC TREATMENTS

The basis of Ayurvedic treatment is dietary. There are several very good Ayurvedic cookbooks on the market, and if you wish to learn more about Ayurvedic nutrition, it would be advisable to buy an appropriate recipe book.

The following pages are divided into sections outlining the basic characteristics of each type: their related emotions, the treatment systems associated with each dosha, and the symptoms of excess, together with information

about what to eat, which colours to wear, the scents and oils to use, the beneficial herbs and spices, and a tonic recipe for each type. Each section also includes a massage, some exercise tips, and an appropriate gem and crystal with which to work in order to help you to reduce any excess in your dosha(s) and also to maintain a balance. The principles are actually very simple, once you have become familiar with them. Follow the relevant plan, whether you are trying to reduce an excess or wish to maintain a balance in your system.

You can make up your own tonic recipes for your body type by combining ingredients from the appropriate eating plan, using recommended herbs and spices to enhance the healing.

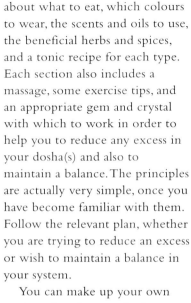

Left: In Ayurveda, the paths of cooking and treatment are intertwined, as certain foods, herbs and spices are used as tonics as well as for prevention and cure. They have a medicinal effect as well as a culinary use.

Left: Vata types benefit from putting some of their energy into creative pursuits.

the business from day to day.

Vata people are artistic, inventive, imaginative and sensitive and would be good in these roles at work. Vata types need regularity, routine, calm and warmth, and should avoid stress, and being ungrounded (avoiding flying or lots of travel, for example).

Pitta people need a challenge and something to develop or engineer without hindrance. They make good salespeople and enjoy developmental occupations, which are well suited to their basic nature.

Kapha people need stimulation and changes of routine to avoid inertia. They make good

Left: Kapha types need to change routines sometimes and have fun.

managers because they are steady and reliable. They will tend always to be there when you need them.

Each individual will have specific qualities to bring to the workplace, and business benefits from finding the right people for the right jobs. The key to a successful company is to employ all three doshic types to ensure a balanced team.

Above: Pitta types need to relax and slow down, taking time to appreciate themselves and others.

DOSHIC QUALITIES
Vata: creative, good ideas
Pitta: activators, good promoters
Kapha: reliable, good managers

THE DOSHAS AT WORK

The differences and interdependencies between the various doshic types can be seen very clearly in a working environment. Here, vata people may produce imaginative ideas, but won't necessarily put them into action. They need pitta people to develop, engineer and sell. But pitta types want to be always active on the leading edge and so need kapha people to run

VATA

THE VATA BODY TYPE IS USUALLY thin and narrow. Vatas do not gain weight easily and are often restless by nature, especially when they are busy and active. They have dry hair and cool skin and a tendency to feel the cold. Their levels of energy are erratic, and they have to be careful not to exhaust themselves due to lack of consistency. They may find it hard to relax, which can lead to an over-active mind and insomnia.

Vata symptoms will be changeable, cold in their nature and therefore worse in cold weather. Any pain will worsen during change. Vata

Left: Vata people should eat warming food which is earthy and sweet, with the emphasis upon cooked foods, such as this bowl of dhal, rather than salads.

people can suffer from wind, low back pain, arthritis and nerve disorders. When there is excess vata in the system, fear, depression and nervousness will develop. Whenever there are repressed emotions, vata will also be aggravated which, in turn, will affect the flora and fauna present in the digestive system, causing not only a degree of discomfort and bloating, but also a lessening of the effectiveness of the immune system.

Vata types, because of their restless nature, require a regular intake of nourishment and should sit down to eat or drink at regular times. Exercise should be in moderation, maintaining a gentle routine that will help to focus the mind and body to work in unison. Routine and regularity help to ground excess vata.

Right: In summer vata is accumulating as the heat of the sun begins to dry everything out. Keep your skin moist with natural creams in order to prevent your skin drying out too.

ELEMENTS: ether and air
CLIMATE: dry and cold
PRINCIPLE: movement
EMOTIONS: fearful, anxious, sensitive, nervous, changeable
SYSTEMS MOST AFFECTED BY EXCESS VATA: the nervous system and the colon
SYMPTOMS OF EXCESS VATA: flatulence, back pain, circulation problems, dry skin, fearfulness, arthritis, constipation and nerve disorders

DIETARY RECOMMENDATIONS

Vata people should avoid all fried foods and should eat at regular intervals. To reduce excess vata, follow the vata diet and recommendations in your eating and living plan and avoid foods and other items not listed as much as possible. If including animal products, these should be used in moderation.

HERBS AND SPICES
Almond essence, asafoetida (hing), basil leaves, bay leaves, black mustard seeds, cardamom

Below: Ginger, cardamom pods, vanilla pods, coriander, oregano, cloves, black mustard seeds and asafoetida (hing).

Above: Wheat grains, pumpkin seeds and long grain rice.

pods, cloves, coriander (cilantro), cumin, dill, fennel, fresh ginger, marjoram, mint, nutmeg, oregano, paprika, parsley, peppermint, spearmint, tarragon, thyme, turmeric and vanilla – of these herbs, asafoetida is especially good for vata types. It helps with the smooth digestion of food and reduces wind, which is particularly useful if you eat pulses and beans.

GRAINS AND SEEDS
Oats (cooked), pumpkin seeds, quinoa, rice (all varieties), sesame seeds, sprouted wheat bread, sunflower seeds and wheat.

NUTS
Almonds, brazil nuts, cashews, hazelnuts, macadamias, pecans, pine nuts, pistachios and walnuts.

MEAT AND FISH
Beef, chicken, duck, eggs, seafish, shrimps and turkey. Vatas may benefit from eating meat and fish because these foods are grounding and strengthening.

VEGETABLES
Artichokes, asparagus, beetroot, carrots, courgettes (zucchini), cucumber, daikon radish, green

Below: Cashews, pine nuts, pecans, almonds and pistachios.

Above: Eggs and mackerel.

beans, leeks, okra, olives, onions (cooked), parsnips, pumpkins, radishes, spinach (cooked), swede (rutabagas), sweet potatoes, tomatoes (cooked) and watercress.

Below: Cow's milk, cottage cheese and goat's cheese.

FRUIT

Apricots, avocados, bananas, berries, cherries, coconuts, dates, fresh figs, grapefruit, grapes, lemons, limes, mangoes, melons, oranges, peaches, pineapples, plums, rhubarb and strawberries.

DAIRY PRODUCTS

Cow's milk, cottage cheese, goat's milk, goat's cheese and soft cheese – all to be taken in moderation.

COOKING OILS

Unrefined sesame oil.

DRINKS

Apricot juice, berry juice, carrot juice, cider, ginger tea, grape juice, grapefruit juice, hot dairy

Below: Unrefined sesame oil.

Above: Carrots, daikon radish, olives, courgettes (zucchini), asparagus, artichokes and watercress.

drinks, lemon balm tea, lemonade, orange juice, peach juice, peppermint tea, pineapple juice, rosehip tea and spearmint

Below: Orange juice.

AROMAS AND MASSAGE OILS

Vata people tend to benefit more than either of the other doshas from massage, and they should consider massaging their feet, hands and head every morning and having a regular massage once a week. Vata aromas are warm and sweet, and the most appropriate massage oil for the vata personality is warmed sesame oil. In general, all oil is good for vata and vata types, and if vata is seriously out of balance, the once-weekly massage may be increased to three times a week.

Essential oils must be diluted. Do not put them directly on your

skin or take them internally. It is advisable not to use the same essential oil for more than two weeks; interchange your essential oils so that you do not create a toxic build-up or overload of one fragrance. If you are pregnant or have a diagnosed medical

Left: Mix 7–10 drops of your chosen essential oil with 25ml/1fl oz/ 1/8 cup carrier oil, and pour oil on to your hands first, to warm it before you begin.

condition, do not use any essential oil without consulting a qualified practitioner.

Warm, calming or earthy essential oils are the most suitable for vata. These include camphor (which can be an irritant, so test yourself for sensitivity first), eucalyptus, ginger, sandalwood and jatamansi (a spikenard species from India).

VATA MASSAGE

1 A vata massage should be gentle.

2 Keep the actions soothing and relaxing.

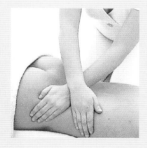

3 Use stroking movements.

4 Oil and ease areas of dry, tight skin.

COLOURS

Vata individuals benefit from most of the pastel colours and from earthy colours that are gentle and warm to look at, such as ochres, browns and yellows.

OCHRE
A warm, friendly but relaxing colour, ochre draws the energy down through the system, helping the vata individual to feel more solid and steady.

BROWN
A solid, reliable colour that helps to ground the vata type, stabilizing any tendency to flightiness, holding the emotions in place, and helping the vata personality to consolidate and concentrate.

YELLOW
A warming, enlivening colour, yellow is linked to the mind and the intellect. It

Right: Warm yellows are suitable for vata people.

helps to keep the vata mentality alert by focusing the mind and calming any rising emotions.

MAKING A COLOUR INFUSION
Take a piece of thin cotton or silk. The fabric should be warm yellow in colour and sufficiently thin to allow the light to penetrate. Wrap it around a small transparent (not coloured) jar or bottle filled with

Above: Make a colour infusion to treat symptoms of excess vata – entering a potentially stressful situation, for example. Choose clothes and accessories that will be warming and comforting.

spring water. Leave it outside in the sunlight for about four hours. Remove the fabric and drink the infusion to encourage a sense of warmth and well-being. Vata infusions should not be stored in the fridge, but kept at room temperature.

GEMS AND CRYSTALS

Gems and crystals have healing qualities that can be utilized in Ayurvedic medicine. Their powers are taken seriously by the jyotish (Vedic astrologer), who can determine which gems or crystals to use depending on the circumstances of your life chart.

Topaz is a warm stone that traditionally dispels fear, making it an ideal stone for vata as it calms emotionalism and anxiety. Wear topaz whenever you want to feel confident and in control. Amethyst is an appropriate crystal to wear when you want to balance vata. It promotes clarity of mind and thought, and will help you to radiate a sense of harmony.

There may be times when it is advisable to remove all crystals – when you find circumstances in your life are changing for the worse. This indicates that your birth chart or constitution does not require the healing qualities of a particular crystal, or that it is highlighting some area of your birth chart in a negative way.

MAKING A CRYSTAL INFUSION

Before making a crystal infusion, it is advisable to cleanse your crystal first. (Crystals that are used for infusions should ideally be cleansed before and after each use.) To make a crystal infusion, take the cleansed crystal and hold it in your hands, imagining that the crystal is full of peace and calm. Place the crystal in a clear glass bowl, cover it with spring water, and leave it in the sunlight for about four hours. Remove the

TOURMALINE QUARTZ

AVENTURINE

MILKY QUARTZ

CITRINE

ROSE QUARTZ

SMOKY QUARTZ

CLEAR QUARTZ

RUTILATED QUARTZ

AMETHYST

Left: Amethyst, from the quartz family, is good for vata. This and other crystals from this family are the safest for infusions.

crystal and bottle the spring water. Drink the infusion prior to any mentally demanding tasks. It will aid clarity of mind and help to reduce any stress that might arise as a result of pressure. You can keep the infusion for 24 hours, after which it should be discarded. Store your infusion away from domestic appliances and electrical equipment.

Right: Amethyst is an ideal healing stone, as it balances and quietens the mind. You may become aware of an increased imagination and a greater ability to visualize clearly.

CLEANSING A CRYSTAL

1 To cleanse your amethyst, dissolve a teaspoon of sea salt in a clear glass bowl filled with spring water.

2 Place the crystal in the water and leave it to stand for about eight hours (or you can leave it overnight).

3 Rinse it in spring water, visualizing any residues that were being held in the crystal being washed away.

EXERCISE AND TONIC

Vata is cold in nature and so benefits from warmth and comfort. Make your own warming tonic drinks for cold windy days by combining ingredients from the vata eating plan. Be aware that sugar weakens the immune system and vatas, with their tendency to stress (another immune suppressor), need to be particularly wary of

Right: Meditation in half or full lotus keeps the spine straight and energy flowing freely.

sugary and refined foods, choosing naturally sweet-tasting foods, such as fruit, instead.

Vata people benefit from gentle, relaxing forms of exercise. They are the most easily exhausted of the various categories, so they should be careful not to overdo things. Examples of gentle exercise include walking, yoga and slow swimming. In essence, it is not so much the form of exercise that you take, but rather the way in which you take it. With vata,

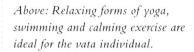

Above: Relaxing forms of yoga, swimming and calming exercise are ideal for the vata individual.

the exercise routine should be gentle; with this in mind, vata types can undertake most sports and activities.

Yoga stretches will gently lengthen your muscles and increase your flexibility. If you do not practise yoga as a form of exercise, you may find that achieving a half or full lotus for meditation is too difficult. If this is the case, you can use a specifically designed meditation stool, or place some firm cushions underneath you. Push your bent knees on to the floor, then tuck your feet in towards you on the floor, forming a solid triangular base with your legs.

FRESH GINGER AND LEMON TEA

This fresh ginger and lemon tea is a delicious tonic for a vata.

1 lemon
A small piece of fresh ginger (about the size of a thumbnail)
Spring water
Raw honey or fructose (fruit sugar)

1 Wash the lemon and then cut it into thin slices, leaving the peel on.

2 Peel the piece of fresh ginger and slice it finely.

3 Place the lemon and ginger slices in a small teapot.

4 Add boiling spring water. Stir. Sweeten with honey or fructose.

PITTA

THE PITTA BODY TYPE IS USUALLY OF average build and nicely proportioned. Pittas like their food and have a healthy appetite. The hair is usually straight, fine and fair (but dark-haired people can also be pitta types). People with red hair will automatically have some level of pitta within their nature. Like the fire element, their temperament can be intense, and when it manifests in excess this can lead to intolerance and irritability.

Pitta skin will have a tendency to be sensitive to the sun, and pitta types will need to be careful how much time they spend in direct

ELEMENTS: fire and water
CLIMATE: hot and moist
PRINCIPLE: transformation
EMOTIONS: hate, anger, intolerance, impatience, jealousy, humour, intelligence, warm-heartedness
SYSTEMS AFFECTED BY EXCESS PITTA: skin, metabolism, small intestines, eyes, liver, hair of the head
SYMPTOMS OF EXCESS PITTA: skin disorders, acidity, sun-sensitivity, premature hair loss or loss of hair colour, diarrhoea

sunlight. The fiery nature of the sun will sometimes inflame the pitta person, leading to skin rashes, freckles and sunburn. All hot and humid weather will aggravate pitta. Cool showers, cool environments and cooling drinks (but not ice-cold ones) will help to alleviate any steaming temperatures and calm pitta down.

People of this nature can be impatient, because their highly active and alert minds can make them aggressive in situations that are irritating to them. However, pitta people can also have a very good sense of humour and a warm personality. They make good promoters and salespeople because they like challenge. It is good for pitta to have the opportunity to rise to a challenge, but they must ensure that after frantic activity some time is dedicated to rest and recuperation, something that pitta types will tend to avoid.

Pitta people should choose foods that are soothing and avoid hot, spicy dishes.

Right: Pitta types benefit from spending time in shaded and naturally calming surroundings.

DIETARY RECOMMENDATIONS

The pitta person should avoid all hot, spicy and sour foods, as they will aggravate this dosha; they should also avoid all fried foods. Any heating of food and drink will increase pitta within the system, so pitta types should eat more raw than cooked foods. As a primarily vegetarian system, Ayurveda does not advocate the eating of animal products, especially for the pitta dosha, so although some meats and other animal products have been included in the following list, they should really be used in strict moderation.

Below: Dill, dried coriander leaves and spearmint.

Above: Sunflower seeds, basmati rice, barley and rice cakes.

To reduce excess pitta in the system (vikruti), or to maintain balance within your personality (prakruti) because you are a pitta type by nature, include the following foods in your eating and living plan, and avoid any items that are not listed as much as you can.

HERBS AND SPICES
Aloe vera juice (not to be used in pregnancy), basil leaves, cinnamon, coriander (cilantro), cumin, dill, dulse, fennel, fresh ginger, hijiki, mint leaves and spearmint.

GRAINS AND SEEDS
Barley, basmati rice, flax seeds, psyllium seeds, rice cakes, sunflower seeds, wheat, wheat bran and white rice.

BEANS AND PULSES
Aduki beans, black beans, black-eyed beans, chickpeas (garbanzos), kidney beans, lentils (red and brown), lima beans, mung beans, pinto beans, soya beans, split peas, tempeh and tofu.

NUTS
Almonds (peeled) and coconuts.

Below: Black-eyed beans, mung beans, soya beans, aduki beans and chickpeas (garbanzos).

Above: Coconut and almonds.

MEAT AND FISH
Chicken, freshwater fish, rabbit, turkey and venison.

VEGETABLES
Artichokes, asparagus, broccoli, Brussels sprouts, butternut squash, cabbages, carrots, cauliflowers, courgettes (zucchini), cucumber, celery, fennel, green beans, green peppers, Jerusalem artichokes, kale, leafy greens, leeks, lettuces, mushrooms, onions (cooked), parsnips, peas, pumpkins, spinach (cooked), swede (rutabagas), sweet potatoes, white potatoes and winter squash. Pittas should eat salads regularly, and eat raw rather than cooked vegetables.

FRUIT
Apples, apricots, avocadoes, berries, cherries, dates, figs,

Above: Melon, mango, avocado, blackberries, apricot, cherries and pineapple.

mangoes, melons, oranges, pears, pineapples, plums, pomegranates, prunes, quinces, raisins, red grapes and watermelons. Always make sure that the fruits are fully ripe, very sweet and fresh.

Below: Walnut oil, sunflower oil, and olive oil.

Above: Unsalted butter, yogurt and cottage cheese.

DAIRY PRODUCTS
Cottage cheese, cow's milk, diluted yogurt, ghee, goat's milk, mild soft cheese and unsalted butter may be consumed in moderation.

COOKING OILS
Olive oil, sunflower oil, soya and walnut oil. As with dairy products, these oils should be used in moderation.

DRINKS
Apple juice, apricot juice, cool dairy drinks, grape juice, mango juice, mixed vegetable juice, soya milk, vegetable bouillon, elderflower tea, hibiscus tea, jasmine tea, marshmallow tea, nettle tea, spearmint tea and strawberry tea. Juices should be cool but not ice-cold.

AROMAS AND MASSAGE OILS

Essential oils for pitta include honeysuckle, jasmine, sandalwood and vetiver. They must be diluted and should never be taken internally. Avoid a toxic build-up by interchanging the oils every two weeks. If you are pregnant or have a diagnosed medical condition, consult a practitioner before using essential oils.

Right: A pitta individual requires only a small amount of oil for massage. Choose a cooling carrier oil, such as coconut oil.

PITTA MASSAGE

1 Mix 7–10 drops of your chosen essential oil with 25ml/1 fl oz/⅛ cup carrier oil.

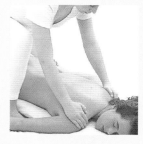

2 Pitta massage should be calming and relaxing. Use deep and varied movements.

3 Be gentle wherever there may be inflamed tissues, such as areas of stiffness or soreness.

4 Use calm, slow, sweeping movements without any sudden changes in direction.

COLOURS

If you are experiencing symptoms of excess pitta, such as irritability or impatience, or on occasions when you know that you are going to have a busy and active day ahead of you, balance your system by wearing natural fibres in cooling and calming colours, such as green, blue, violet or any quiet pastel shade.

BLUE

Blue is a soothing, healing colour which is ideal for the active pitta type. Blue is linked to spiritual consciousness and helps the pitta type to remain open and calm without being over-stimulated.

GREEN

Green, an integral colour of the natural world, brings harmonious feelings to the pitta personality, having the ability to soothe emotions and calm passionate feelings.

Right: Wear blues in silks and cottons.

VIOLET

Violet is a refined colour that soothes and opens the mind, and increases awareness of spiritual issues.

MAKING A COLOUR INFUSION

Take a piece of thin, translucent cotton or silk in violet or light blue. Wrap it

Above: A blue colour infusion will help to clear the system of pressure build-up.

around a small transparent (not coloured) bottle or jar filled with spring water. Leave it outside in dappled sunlight, not in direct sun, for six hours. Remove the fabric, and drink the infusion to encourage the sensation of peace and harmony.

GEMS AND CRYSTALS

When you want to reduce excess pitta, wear pearls or a mother-of-pearl ring set in silver upon the ring finger of your right hand. Pearls have the ability to reduce inflammatory conditions, including heated emotions. Ideally, natural pearls should be worn, although cultured pearls are acceptable. The most harmonious day to put on your pearls is a Monday (the moon's day) during a new moon. Do not wear pearls when you have a kapha condition, such as a cold.

The moonstone has the ability to calm emotions and is soft and cooling, being feminine in orientation. It can help to pacify the pitta personality.

Above: Moonstone is a suitable crystal to use when you need to reduce excess pitta.

MAKING A MOONSTONE INFUSION

1 Take a stone specimen that has already been cleansed. Put it into a clear glass bowl and fill it with fresh spring water until the stone is covered.

2 Leave the bowl outside to stand under the light of a full moon for three hours – or overnight if the night is calm and clear.

3 Remove the moonstone (remember to cleanse it after use) and pour the liquid into a clear glass.

4 Drink the moonstone infusion first thing in the morning, to assure yourself of a harmonious day.

EXERCISE AND TONIC

Cooling drinks such as fruit and vegetable juices are ideal tonics for the pitta constitution.

Pittas require a moderate amount of exercise, which should involve some element of vigour and challenge – jogging, team sports and certain martial arts. It is not so much what you do but how you do it that is important here. Pitta exercise should not over-stimulate the body; any exercise should be kept in line with an average amount of effort and challenge. You should avoid going to such extremes that your pitta nature gets carried away and you overdo it!

Below: Pittas should play games for enjoyment rather than to win.

ORANGE AND ELDERFLOWER INFUSION

This orange and elderflower infusion is a light and delicate alternative to a cordial. Cordials are made by boiling the ingredients together, which is not appropriate for pitta types because of the heat required for the process.

1 large sweet orange
2 large fresh elderflower heads
Fresh spearmint
300ml/½ pint spring water
Fructose (fruit sugar) to taste

1 Wash the orange in spring water. Cut into slices and place in a tall jug.

2 Add the elderflower heads and a sprig of spearmint.
3 Pour in spring water, stir gently and leave it to stand for one hour.
4 Stir again, strain and add fructose to taste.
5 Top with sprigs of fresh spearmint, and sip slowly.

KAPHA

The kapha body type is well built, with a tendency to weight problems, especially if an exercise programme is not followed to keep the kapha active and moving. Kapha people are naturally athletic but need motivation. They are sensitive and emotional and require understanding, otherwise they tend to turn to food as an emotional support. They should ensure that what they eat is suitable for their body type.

Their hair will be thick, fine and wavy, their skin smooth, and their eyes large and attractive.

ELEMENTS: water and earth
CLIMATE: cold and damp
PRINCIPLE: cohesion
EMOTIONS: stubbornness, greed, jealousy, possessiveness, lethargy, reliability and methodical behaviour, kindliness, motherliness
SYSTEMS MOST AFFECTED BY EXCESS KAPHA: joints, lymphatics, body fluids and mucous membranes throughout the body
SYMPTOMS OF EXCESS KAPHA: congestion, bronchial/nasal discharge, sluggish digestion, nausea, slow mental responses, idleness, desire for sleep, excess weight, fluid retention

Above: Kapha food should be light, dry, hot and stimulating. Opt for cooked foods, such as this hot and spicy vegetable curry, in preference to salads.

Kapha people are inclined to be slow and steady, methodical and pragmatic, with a dislike of change. They make good managers, because they like to be reliable and available. They act like an anchor in a business, as they have an innate organizing ability.

Bright, strong and invigorating colours will help to reduce excess kapha and stimulate a system that may be sluggish and dull.

Right: Because kapha individuals have a tendency towards inertia, they need motivation, so early morning exercise outdoors is a good start to the day.

DIETARY RECOMMENDATIONS

Kapha people should focus upon cooked food, but can have some salads occasionally. They should avoid fats and oils, unless these are hot and spicy. Dairy products, sweet, sour and salty tastes and an excessive intake of wheat will also aggravate kapha. Although some meats and animal products have been included, they should really be used in strict moderation.

To reduce excess kapha (vikruti), or to maintain balance because you are a kapha dosha (prakruti), include the following items in your eating plan and try to avoid foods not listed.

Below: Buckwheat, couscous, barley and pumpkin seeds.

Below: Black-eyed beans, aduki beans and chickpeas (garbanzos).

HERBS AND SPICES
Asafoetida (hing), black pepper or pippali (an Indian pepper), chilli pepper, coriander leaves (cilantro), dry ginger, garlic, horseradish, mint leaves, mustard, onions, parsley, radishes or any other hot spices. (Hot spices should be avoided if you suffer from gastro intestinal ulcers.)

GRAINS AND SEEDS
Barley, buckwheat, corn, couscous, oat bran, polenta, popcorn (plain), rye, sprouted wheat bread, toasted pumpkin seeds and toasted sunflower seeds. As the fat content in nuts is high,

this is a food that should be avoided by kapha types. However, toasted seeds, eaten in small quantities, can be used instead of nuts. To toast seeds, place them on a baking tray and put under a hot grill for a few moments, until the seeds start to brown. Shake the tray out occasionally to ensure that the seeds are browned evenly. Toasted seeds are a delicious addition to couscous, and can be sprinkled as a topping over other cooked foods and salads.

BEANS AND PULSES
Aduki beans, black-eyed beans, chickpeas (garbanzos), lima beans,

Below: Eggs and shrimps.

pinto beans, red lentils, split peas and tempeh.

MEAT AND FISH
Eggs, freshwater fish, turkey, rabbit, shrimps and venison.

VEGETABLES
Most kapha vegetables should be cooked. Artichokes, asparagus, aubergines (eggplant), beetroot, broccoli, Brussels sprouts, cabbage, carrots, cauliflower, celery, daikon radish, fennel, green beans, Jerusalem artichokes, kale, leeks, lettuce, mushrooms, okra, onions, peas, peppers, radishes, spinach, swede (rutabagas), sweetcorn, turnips, watercress and white potatoes.

Below: Apples, prunes, cranberries, apricots and pomegranates.

Above: Artichokes, mushrooms, onions, asparagus, green beans and runner beans.

FRUITS
Apples, apricots, berries, cherries, cranberries, peaches, pears, pomegranates, prunes and raisins.

Below: Almond, sunflower and corn oil.

COOKING OILS
Corn, almond or sunflower oil may be used in small quantities.

DRINKS
Fruit drinks should not contain sugar or additives. If you are buying juices from a retail outlet, ensure that the ingredients are fresh and contain no additives or sweeteners. Sweeteners include sugar substitutes, such as saccharin. Hot drinks that are recommended for kapha include black tea, carrot juice, cranberry juice, grape juice, mango juice, mixed vegetable juice, nettle tea, passionflower tea, raspberry tea and wine (a very small amount of dry red or white).

Below: Carrot juice and cranberry juice.

AROMAS AND MASSAGE OILS

Kapha individuals require minimal oil or none at all with massage, using instead a natural, unscented talcum powder which can be purchased from most health food stores. If an essential oil is used at all, the ones that are good for kapha individuals include eucalyptus, cinnamon, orange peel (this can cause sun sensitivity, so avoid strong sunlight after a massage with orange peel), ginger and myrrh. All of these oils are stimulating

Above: If you are going to use essential oils, choose a stimulating one such as ginger, diluting it in a base of almond oil to avoid burning. However, a natural talcum powder is more suitable.

and it would be advisable, after diluting approximately 7–10 drops of essential oil in 25ml/1 fl oz/⅛ cup carrier oil, to test an area of skin first for sensitivity.

Essential oils must be diluted and should not be taken internally. It is advisable not to use the same essential oil for more than two weeks. If you are pregnant or have a diagnosed medical condition, do not use any essential oil without consulting a qualified practitioner.

KAPHA MASSAGE

1 Kapha massage needs to be fairly vigorous, to stimulate a sluggish metabolism and encourage regularity.

2 Use fast and strong movements, using very little oil or none at all – use natural talcum powder instead.

3 Massage that encourages lymphatic drainage is often beneficial, so focus on the hip and groin area.

4 Another major lymph gland area is around the armpits. Massaging here releases any congestion.

COLOURS

Kapha individuals benefit from the warm and stimulating colours of the spectrum.

Whenever you experience symptoms such as lethargy and sluggishness, which suggest excess kapha, or if you need to be particularly active, wear bright, invigorating colours. You will feel more inspired when you wear colours that tend to enliven the kapha personality.

RED
Red is the colour of blood and will increase circulation as well as being energizing and positive. It should be used sparingly, to avoid over-stimulation of kapha, which would then lead to excess pitta.

ORANGE
Orange is a warming, nourishing colour which feeds the sexual organs. Its glowing colour helps to remove congestion in the system.

Right: Boost energy with pink accessories.

PINK
Warm, comforting pinks gently stimulate kapha into activity. Being a softer colour than red, pink may be worn without ill-effect for longer periods.

MAKING A COLOUR INFUSION
Take a piece of thin cotton or silk. The fabric should be naturally dyed to a warm pink and sufficiently translucent to allow the light to penetrate.

Above: A pink colour infusion will help to bring love and warmth into your day.

Wrap it around a transparent (not coloured) small bottle containing spring water. Stand it in full sunlight or upon a windowsill with the window open so that the light can fall naturally upon the bottle, and leave it for about four hours. Remove the fabric and drink the contents of the bottle. You can store the infusion for up to 24 hours, after which it should be discarded.

GEMS AND CRYSTALS

Lapis lazuli is a suitable crystal with which to reduce excess kapha. Known as the heavenly stone, it will help kapha individuals to raise their bodily vibrations, from their tendency to be dense and slow to a more refined and spiritual resonance.

CRYSTAL INFUSION
Cleanse your lapis lazuli prior to making an infusion. Hold the lapis in your hands for a few moments, visualizing clarity and inspiration. The crystal is now ready for use. Place it in a clear glass bowl and cover with spring water. Leave it outside in the sunlight for about four hours. Remove the crystal and bottle the infused spring water. Drink small amounts throughout the day to ensure a continued rising of your spirits towards enlivened and motivated action.

Below: Ruby is a suitable gem to use to reduce excess kapha. Wear a ruby set in gold or silver, to encourage strength and resolve.

Above: Make a lapis infusion to reduce excess kapha.

Right: Garnet pebble.

Right: Polished ruby crystal.

Left: Section of ruby crystal.

EXERCISE AND TONIC

Kapha types may well avoid this page because it suggests exercise! However, kapha people must address their natural aversion to physical activity – it will make all the difference to cleansing excess kapha and so make room for their inner beauty to shine through.

Left: Kapha people need to ensure that they have vigorous exercise, such as aerobics.

SPICED YOGI TEA

Spiced yogi tea is a delicious, warming drink which will help to reduce excess kapha.

1/2 teaspoon dry ginger
4 whole cardamom pods
5 cloves
1 large cinnamon stick
A pinch of black pepper or pippali (Indian long pepper)
600ml/1 pint/2 1/2 cups spring water
30ml/2tbsp goat's milk or organic soya milk

1 Mix the spices together in a saucepan.
2 Add the spring water and boil off half the liquid.
3 Turn off the heat and add the goat's milk or soya milk.
4 Stir and strain the liquid. Serve hot.

Kapha individuals will tend to shy away from vigorous exercise and so a certain amount of self-discipline is required. Once a regular exercise routine is established, however, the kapha type will enjoy and benefit from the enlivened and energetic feeling that activity and exercise brings. Examples of vigorous exercise suited to the kapha type include running, fast swimming, aerobics and fitness training. If unused to exercise, start with a gentle routine, and seek guidance from a qualified trainer.

It is advisable to increase the level of exercise in colder weather when extra stimulation is required, and this should take the form of a regular routine which really pushes the kapha type.

DUAL DOSHAS

IF WHEN YOU ANSWER THE questionnaire discussed earlier, you find that you score twice as many points on any one type as on the other two, this means that you will be predominantly that type. For example, a score of 30

Below: Vata/pitta – pitta/vata herbs include basil, coriander (cilantro), cumin seeds, fennel, mint, turmeric and vanilla pods.

points on kapha and 5 or 10 on the others would indicate that you are a kapha type. If there is a closer gap – perhaps 30 points for kapha and 20 for pitta – you would be a kapha/pitta type.

If you are a dual type, read the following information.

VATA/PITTA – PITTA/VATA
Vata/pitta is a combination of ether/air and fire/water elements.

Below: Eat sweet, ripe fruits such as melons and oranges, when in season, if you are a vata/ pitta type.

If you belong to this dual type, refer to both the vata and the pitta eating and living plans. Choose items from the pitta plan during the spring and summer months and during hot, humid weather. Follow the vata plan during the autumn and winter months and during cold, dry weather. For example, pungent foods aggravate pitta, but can help to calm vata (because vata is cold), which is why the plans need to be changed in accordance with weather, your health or other factors.

Eat your vegetables in season, and mostly cooked and flavoured with appropriate vata spices to minimize aggravation of vata and pitta. Only small amounts of bitter vegetables should be used. Among foods suitable for the vata/pitta type are broccoli, cauliflower, cucumber, endive, kale, onion (cooked), plantain, coconut, sweet oranges, apricots and other sweet fruits. Teas that are beneficial include elderflower, fennel, lemon balm and rosehip teas. Herbs and spices for vata/pitta – pitta/vata include fresh basil, caraway, cardamom, cumin, fennel, garam masala, spearmint and vanilla.

The nature of vata is change and so for this reason, when you become more familiar with

Right: Fennel is useful for digestive disorders.

the doshic influences that the climate has upon you as an individual, you may want to be more flexible with the doshic recommendations. Remember that it is not only climate that affects the doshas, but absolutely everything that touches your life.

In working and personal relationships, try to adopt the approach recommended for your dosha. If you are a vata dosha, your moods may fluctuate, and

Above: Your lifestyle can be affected by your health. Pitta or vata doshas should find time to create a calming and restful ambience to relax and wind down.

you need to try to approach things with more consistency. If you are a pitta dosha you may get irritated and be abrupt, so do your best to be tolerant and patient. If you are a kapha dosha you may be stubborn, possessive and jealous. Try to be more trusting and flexible.

PITTA/KAPHA – KAPHA/PITTA

This is a combination of fire, water and earth elements. If you are this dual type, follow the kapha eating and living plan during the winter months and during cold, damp weather

Below: Pitta/kapha – kapha/pitta foods include curry leaves or powder, garam masala, mint, orange peel oil and rosewater.

and follow the pitta plan during the summer months and hot humid weather.

Choose foods that are pungent and astringent, such as onions, celery, lemons, dandelion, mustard greens and watercress, and eat your fruit and vegetables fresh and in season. All fruit juices should be diluted in water or milk. Suitable teas for the pitta/kapha – kapha/pitta type include bancha twig, blackberry,

Above and left: Pitta/kapha vegetables include celery and onion.

dandelion, jasmine, licorice (not to be used if you suffer from high blood pressure or oedema) and spearmint. Herbs, spices and flavourings for the pitta/kapha type include coriander, dill leaves, fennel, kudzu, orange peel, parsley, rosewater and spearmint.

VATA/KAPHA – KAPHA/VATA

Vata/kapha is a combination of ether, air, water and earth. You should follow the kapha eating and living plan during the winter and spring months and in cold, damp weather, and follow the vata plan in the autumn and summer months, and during cold, dry windy spells.

The vata/kapha type is cold and can therefore have plenty of pungent, hot and spicy foods. Examples of suitable foods include artichokes, asparagus,

mustard greens, parsnips, summer and winter squashes and watercress. Vegetables with seeds should be well cooked with the appropriate vata spices to minimize aggravation. Fresh seasonal fruits can be eaten, including apricots, berries, cherries, lemons, mangoes, peaches and strawberries. The vata/kapha type should avoid a mono-diet of brown rice. Herbs and spices for this type include allspice, anise, asafoetida (hing), black pepper, cinnamon, cloves, curry powder, garlic, nutmeg, poppy seeds, saffron and vanilla.

TRIDOSHA

In very rare instances a person may score more or less equally for all three doshas, revealing themselves to be all three types or "tridosha". If you are a combination of all three doshas you will require a tridoshic diet and living plan. Follow the seasonal changes and eat according to the

Right: Use cloves and cinnamon to flavour hot, spicy dishes and warming drinks.

weather or your personal circumstances. On hot days, and during the spring and summer months, follow the pitta plan; on cold days and during the winter months, follow the kapha plan; and during the late summer and autumn or on windy

Above: Vata/kapha – kapha/vata herbs and spices include asafoetida, allspice, curry powder, peppercorns, curry leaves, nutmeg, cinnamon, cloves and vanilla pods.

days or in cold dry weather follow the vata plan.

If you find that you fall into this unusual category, it is advisable to consult an Ayurvedic practitioner to find out more about tridosha.

Ayurvedic Self-help in the Home

Before you begin to read this section, or consider treating yourself for a complaint, note that it is *vitally important* that pregnant women, children, or anyone who has severe health problems, or uses prescription medicine, should consult an Ayurvedic physician or other doctor before using any Ayurvedic herbs or other treatments.

In Ayurvedic medicine you always treat a condition with its opposite. For a burn, for example, which is hot and dry, you would

Below: The gel from aloe vera can be used to treat minor burns.

administer something cool and moist, such as the gel from the leaves of an aloe vera plant. Ayurveda does not treat the condition, it treats the pattern of the body type. This means that there will be three different types

Above: Heat and steam is a remedy for certain kapha conditions as it acts as a powerful stimulus.

of treatment, according to whether the condition is vata, pitta or kapha in nature. Vata

Right: Tai chi is particularly therapeutic for the pitta dosha.

symptoms will be changeable, arising from tension and stress. They should be treated with relaxation, warmth and calm. Pitta conditions will be hot and intense, and are related to the liver, arising from suppressed anger or frustration. They should be treated with cool, relaxing things that help to release the suppressions. Kapha conditions will be dull and congestive.

Some conditions may be vata, pitta or kapha, according to the symptoms, while others are generally linked with one dosha. Diarrhoea, for example, is a pitta condition, and constipation is a vata one. When referring to the following information, you will

Below: Gentle yoga is suitable for vata people.

need to discover whether your condition is displaying vata, pitta or kapha symptoms. You can then turn to the relevant vata, pitta or kapha section and follow the outlined plan for treatment to reduce the excess in that

particular dosha, which is irritating the condition.

You should lessen the recommended treatments when symptoms subside, especially the Ayurvedic herbs or spices. However, if you are a particular doshic type with a condition from the same dosha, maintain the appropriate plan with moderate use of the herbs and spices. Remember that some conditions will require proper medical treatment. Diarrhoea, for example, can cause serious loss of body fluids and tissue salts, especially if vomiting is involved as well. Be sensible with your self-help regime and always consult a qualified Ayurvedic or medical doctor if your condition either worsens or fails to respond to the treatment.

SELF-MASSAGE FOR YOUR DOSHA

All dosha types benefit from massage. Vata people, and others who have dry skin, should always use oil for massage. The pitta dosha can be over-stimulated if too much oil is used, so just enough should be applied to avoid dragging the skin. Any kind of massage helps to provide the stimulation a kapha body requires, but deep-tissue massage is especially useful in aiding waste disposal via the lymph system. You can choose an oil purely because it is suitable for your skin type. But if you feel that you are suffering from an excess of one of your energies – light-headed vata, for example, or impatient pitta – choose an appropriate oil for your dosha. Take outside influences into account: if it is a damp evening in spring, for example, kapha energy will already be high.

HAIR OIL FOR YOUR DOSHA

Vata's typically dry hair will revel in the luxury of black sesame oil. Pitta needs very gentle massage with brahmi oil or coconut oil,

OIL ESSENTIALS

In Ayurvedic practice, oil is believed to help clear toxicity (*ama*) out of the body. It also reduces excess dosha, which is considered to stick like a solid substance until softened and flushed out in the form of bodily secretions. Oil should be washed off after a treatment, so any waste products released into it do not re-enter the body.

to stimulate the scalp without damaging the follicles. These two oils are good for all hair types. If you are kapha, good hair is your

birthright but it may be prone to excess oil. Use sesame or mustard oil, but leave it on for only 30–60 minutes before showering it off.

Ayurveda recommends self-massage each morning. As you massage, vary your touch so that you are sometimes moving your hands lightly over the skin, and at other times pressing firmly to move the skin over the bone. Use the fingertips for static pressure, but the softer pads of the fingers for kneading or circling movements. Avoid putting pressure on joints, and any pressure should be upwards, towards the head. Always warm the oil and ensure the room is pleasantly warm. Start by pouring a little oil into one palm and rubbing your hands together. Repeat this as the oil wears off your hands. If you prefer not to get oil in your hair, you can do the head massage without.

Left: Traditionally, Indian women regularly treat their hair with oil.

HEAD AND SHOULDER MASSAGE

1 Press your hands against your scalp and move the skin in large circles. Use fingertips and thumbs to make small circles all over your head.

2 Smooth oil into your neck and work it up over the back of your head. Cup the base of the skull in your palms and press gently upwards.

3 Run well-oiled palms in long strokes up your throat from the collarbones, covering the front and sides; repeat several times.

4 Cup your chin in each palm in turn and run the fingers along the jawline several times. Use firm pressure without dragging the skin.

5 Massage your forehead and cheeks in small circles with your fingertips. Keep the movement upwards and outwards.

6 Massage the scalp and the base of the skull in small circles. Then rub and squeeze the ears and massage all around them.

7 Relax your shoulders and let your head sink forwards. Place your palms on the back of your neck and rub out to the sides.

8 Rub oil into each shoulder, using your whole palm and fingers. Rotate the joints gently if there is any stiffness.

THE GASTRO-INTESTINAL TRACT

In Ayurvedic medicine, the gastro-intestinal tract (GI) is the most important part of the body, as it is thought to be the seat of the doshas. Vata is formed in the colon, pitta in the small intestine and kapha in the stomach.

CONSTIPATION

Drink warm liquids; hot water is acceptable, but not chilled water. Herbs for constipation are triphala and satisabgol (psyllium husks). (Do not use triphala if

VATA AND THE GASTRO-INTESTINAL TRACT
Regular daily bowel movements are a sign of a healthy GI. Typical vata conditions of the GI include constipation, gas/flatulence, and tension – cramps or spasms, such as irritable bowel syndrome.

Above: Eating a healthy vata diet can aid vata problems associated with the gastro-intestinal tract.

you are pregnant or suffering from ulcers of the GI.) Triphala is a combination of three herbal fruits, each of which has a rejuvenating effect in relation to one of the doshas. Satisabgol is a demulcent laxative. It is gentle and soothing and holds moisture in the colon, thus helping vata, which is dry and cold. Satisabgol can be used with triphala, as they complement one another.

GAS, BLOATING, COLIC

These symptoms are usually related to constipation. Ideally food should pass through the system in 24 hours. If left for

much longer there is fermentation, which causes a build-up of gas. The herbal remedy for this is hingvastak, a mix of asafoetida (hing), pippali, ginger, black pepper, cumin, wild celery seeds and rock salt.

A massage with brahmi oil – a medicated oil that is used to restore and relax the nervous system – is another traditional Ayurvedic remedy.

Below: When massaging, follow the direction of the colon – from lower left, across the abdomen, up to the right and across to the left.

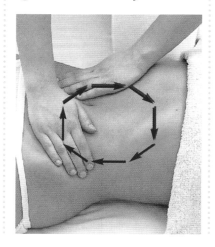

Above: Nettle tea is very good at balancing the digestive system and can help to alleviate pitta conditions such as diarrhoea.

ACIDITY/HEARTBURN

Sip aloe vera juice (without any citric acid added). Add fresh and dried coriander (cilantro), turmeric, saffron, coconut, fennel or peppermint to your diet. Shatavari *(Asparagus racemosus)*, licorice (not to be used with high blood pressure or oedema) and amalaki are used in Ayurveda to balance acidity.

DIARRHOEA

Pitta diarrhoea is generally hot, and often yellowish and foul-smelling. Diarrhoea is mainly related to pitta but can sometimes be caused by other factors, such as high toxicity (ama), stress or emotional factors. Persistent symptoms must be dealt with by a physician.

If you have diarrhoea, avoid hot spices and follow the pitta plan. Eat abstemiously if at all, drinking plenty of fluids and adding coriander (cilantro), saffron and a little cardamom, fresh ginger and nutmeg to your diet. A simple diet of rice, split mung dhal and vegetables is most suitable for the pitta dosha, while symptoms last.

Below: Vegetables for the pitta diet.

PITTA AND THE GASTRO-INTESTINAL TRACT

Pitta digestion tends to be fast and "burns" food. This is made worse by anger or frustration. Begin a pitta-reducing diet and eat in a calm and relaxed way. Typical pitta conditions of the gastro-intestinal tract include acidity and heartburn, symptomized by belching and acid indigestion; diarrhoea or frequent loose bowel movements, and constant hunger, accompanied by consequent irritability.

PERSISTENT HUNGER/INCREASED APPETITE

In general, follow the pitta plan and use aloe vera juice as above. Increase relaxation, meditation and yoga. Have a massage with brahmi oil. If strong symptoms persist, consult your physician.

KAPHA AND THE GASTRO-INTESTINAL TRACT

Typical kapha conditions of the GI include poor appetite – kapha tends to be low in *agni* (digestive fire), which can create a slow metabolism and weight gain; nausea; a build-up of mucus, leading to colds, sinus problems, coughs and flu; and poor circulation, resulting in a build-up of toxicity (ama). Follow the kapha plan and eat plenty of hot spices, such as chilli peppers, garlic, ginger and black pepper, until the condition clears, after which you should reduce your intake of hot spices. Herbs for kapha conditions of the GI include trikatu ("three hot things"), to be taken or added to meals. This contains pippali, ginger and black pepper. You should also have plenty of vigorous exercise.

NAUSEA

Ginger and cardamom tea will often calm nausea. To make it, peel and thinly slice a piece of fresh ginger, add five cardamom pods and pour boiled spring water over them. Leave to stand for five minutes and drink while still hot.

Ginger is a carminative and a stimulant. This means that it has the ability to combat intestinal bloating and to speed processes in the GI so that balance is restored. During the winter and spring, when kapha is seasonally high, dried ginger can be blended with some boiled spring water and a little honey to help keep the digestive system active and moving, so helping to reduce the

Right: Ginger root.

Below: Ginger and cardamom tea.

Above: Hot kapha dietary spices.

risk of colds, coughs and flu.

Cardamom (common in Southern India as well as other tropical areas) can be used for kapha and vata digestive conditions, although only in small amounts as it can aggravate pitta or bring about a pitta excess. As with all the recommended foods, herbs and spices, the purer the quality, the more beneficial they will be. Therefore, try to buy organic herbs and spices when possible.

COMMON PROBLEMS

The forms taken by commonly occurring illnesses and the appropriate remedies will vary according to whether you have a vata, pitta or kapha dosha.

INSOMNIA
Any vata-increasing influence can contribute to insomnia, including lots of travel, stress, an irregular or ungrounded lifestyle and the use of stimulants such as tea and coffee. The herbs used to treat vata-based insomnia are brahmi (*Centella*), jatamansi, ashwagandha (*Withania somnifera*) and nutmeg. A massage using brahmi oil will be beneficial.

Below: A foot massage with brahmi oil may relieve insomnia.

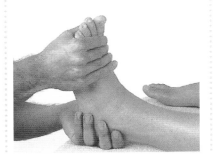

Above: Juice from aloe vera plants can combat sleeplessness.

Insomnia in the pitta dosha is brought on by anger, jealousy, frustration, fever, excess sun or heat. Follow the pitta plan, which is cooling, and take brahmi, jatamansi, bhringaraj (*Eclipta alba*), shatavari and aloe vera juice. Massage brahmi oil into the head and feet.

As kapha types like to sleep and tend to be sleepy, they rarely suffer from insomnia.

HEADACHE/MIGRAINE
Vata headaches cause extreme pain and are related to anxiety and tension. Treatments include triphala to clear any congestion, jatamansi, brahmi and calamus.

Pitta headaches are associated with heat or burning sensations, flushed skin and visual sensitivity to light. They are related to anger, frustration or irritability, and will be connected to the liver and gall bladder. Treatments are brahmi, turmeric and aloe vera juice.

Kapha headaches are dull and heavy and can cause nausea. There may also be congestion, such as catarrh. Have a stimulating massage, with minimal oil, and take plenty of exercise to alleviate congestion.

Below: Massage the head with sandalwood, coconut or brahmi oil for pitta insomnia.

COLDS

A tendency to mucus production or catarrh/phlegm is usually due to poor digestion of foods in the stomach which increases ama (toxicity) and kapha. In general, kapha is the main dosha involved.

Vata-type colds involve dry symptoms, such as a dry cough or dry throat. Herbs for vata coughs and colds are ginger, cumin, pippali, tulsi (holy basil, *Ocimum*

Below: Adding puréed spearmint leaves to a bowl of warm water makes a soothing footbath for pitta-type colds.

sanctum), cloves and peppermint, licorice (not to be used with high blood pressure or oedema), shatavari and ashwagandha. Put one or two drops of sesame oil up each nostril and follow the vata plan until symptoms subside.

Pitta-type colds involve more heat, the face is usually red and there may even be a fever. The mucus is often yellow and can contain blood. Herbs for pitta coughs and colds are peppermint and other mints, sandalwood, chrysanthemum and a little tulsi. Follow the pitta plan until symptoms subside.

Above: Spiced hot lemon tea for kapha colds.

Kapha colds are thick and mucusy, with a feeling of heaviness in the head and/or body. Avoid cold, damp weather and exposure to cold and damp conditions. Eliminate sugar, refined foods, meat and nuts, dairy products, bread, fats and oils from the diet and use plenty of hot spices. Drink a spiced tea of hot lemon, ginger and cinnamon with cloves or tulsi, sweetened with a little raw honey. Herbs for kapha colds are ginger, cinnamon, pippali, tulsi, cloves and peppermint. Saunas and hot baths will help to increase the heat of the kapha person, but they should not be used in excess as this would increase pitta too much. Follow the kapha plan until symptoms subside.

COUGHS

Vata coughs are dry and irritated with very little mucus, the chief symptom being a painful cough often accompanied by a dry mouth. Herbs and spices for the vata cough include licorice (do not use this if you have high blood pressure or oedema), shatavari, ashwagandha and cardamom. Follow the vata plan until the symptoms subside.

Below: It is worth having a supply of fresh mint and other herbs to hand for many of the common Ayurvedic treatments.

Above: Cardamom pods are beneficial to vata-type coughs.

Pitta coughs are usually associated with a lot of phlegm. The chest is congested, but the mucus cannot be brought up properly. There is often fever or heat, combined with a burning sensation in the chest or throat. High fevers should be treated by a physician, and people with asthma should consult their doctor immediately if a cough or cold leads to wheezing and difficult breathing. The best herbs for pitta coughs include peppermint, tulsi and sandalwood. Follow the pitta plan until the symptoms have completely subsided.

With kapha coughs, the patient usually brings up lots of phlegm, and suffers a loss of appetite combined with nausea. The chest is loaded with mucus, but this may not be coughed up because the kapha individual is likely to feel tired. Treatments for kapha coughs are raw honey, lemon, cloves and chyawanprash (a herbal jam). Follow the kapha plan until the symptoms subside, increasing your intake of hot spices, and use trikatu powder. Keep warm and avoid damp, cold environments.

SKIN PROBLEMS

These are often caused by internal conditions of toxicity (ama) and are mainly related to the pitta dosha.

Vata skin problems will be dry and rough. Avoid letting the skin dry out, and exposing it to cold and/or windy weather. Herbal remedies for vata skin are triphala and satisabgol (the latter is also useful if you are constipated).

Pitta skin problems will be red, swollen, raised or inflamed, often with a yellow head or yellow pus discharge. Avoid sun, heat or hot baths, and increase your intake of salads, raw vegetables and fruits.

Follow the pitta plan and add turmeric, coriander and saffron to your diet. The remedies for pitta skin problems are manjishta (*Rubia cordifolia*), kutki (*Picrohiza kurroa*), neem (*Azadirachta indica*), turmeric and aloe vera juice.

Kapha skin problems will involve congestion in the blood, which can cause the skin to form thick and mucusy whiteheads. Increase your level of exercise, and follow the kapha plan. Treatments for kapha skin conditions include a small amount of calamus, cinnamon, cloves, dry ginger, trikatu formula and turmeric.

Above: Fresh fruit is suitable for pitta skin conditions.

Left: Fresh figs are recommended for the vata diet.

Below: Cloves for kapha problems.

URINARY INFECTIONS

The kidneys are very important in Ayurvedic medicine. In the West, we tend to overburden our kidneys by the use of diuretics. In Ayurveda the body is considered to be chiefly made up of plasma rather than water. Excess cold water, tea, coffee, and alcoholic drinks will weaken the kidneys. Salt, sugar or foods that are rich in calcium, such as dairy products or spinach, will similarly tend to weaken and toxify the kidneys. The best kidney tonic to use in Ayurveda is shilajit, a mineral-rich compound from the Himalayan mountains, but this should be avoided if you suffer from kidney stones.

Below: Add cinnamon to your diet to relieve kapha-type cystitis.

Above: Lime and coconut are recommended for pitta cystitis.

Pregnant women, children or those on medication should consult an Ayurvedic practitioner before treatment.

CYSTITIS

In vata people, cystitis will tend to be less intense. Remedies are shilajit (to be avoided if you suffer from kidney stones) with bala (*Sida cordifolia*), ashwagandha and shatavari.

Cystitis is mainly a pitta condition because it burns and is hot and inflamed. Follow the pitta plan, using plenty of coriander (cilantro) and avoiding hot food and spices. Remedies are aloe vera juice (not to be used in pregnancy), lime juice, coconut, coriander, pomegranate, punarnava (*Boerrhaavia diffusa*), shilajit and sandalwood.

Kapha-type cystitis is accompanied by congestion and mucus in the urinary tract, and the urine is often pale or clear. The treatments are cinnamon, trikatu combined with shilajit, gokshura (*Tribulis terrestris*) and gokshurdi guggul.

COLOUR HEALING

*Colour is a subconscious language, it is all around us
and affects our behaviour on many levels – emotionally,
physically and psychologically. We might describe
someone as having a black humour, or say that
we are feeling blue, for example. Colour is a positive
source of energy and this chapter demonstrates how
its power can be used to promote harmony and well-being.*

COLOUR HEALING PRINCIPLES

WE ARE SWAMPED WITH COLOUR from the moment we are born. Indeed, we are born into a specific colour that stays with us for life. Colour is an aspect of everything we eat, drink, touch and are surrounded by. We use colours to describe our physical health, attitudes, emotions and even our spiritual or psychic experiences. Colour is an intimate part of our being, even though most of the time we take it for granted. However, it is impossible to be indifferent to colour. It affects every home environment, as well as those of factories, offices, schools and hospitals. Even the colours of your clothes reflect your personality and influence your mood, and colour has a practical bearing on all your personal relationships. Without light there is no life. If you put a plant in a dark cupboard, it will wither and die. Light is a natural requisite for growth and life, and, as living beings, we are continually reacting to the wide range of stimuli that we call light. From light come all the colours, each, as we will see in the following pages, with its own impact upon our systems.

Many of our healing needs can be met by the use of colour to bring about harmony and balance within the psyche and the body. The invisible vibrations of colour can either relax or stimulate us according to the colours chosen for healing. Even blind people can develop a sense of colour, by allowing the fingers to pick up the vibrational energy of different colours.

Looking closely at colour is a non-invasive way of discovering yourself. Its power is both transcendent and intuitive. Get to know what colour can do for you. Do not delay or neglect responding to this inner knowledge – colour can change your life.

Left: Recharge your will and stamina by meditating on the ruby red petals of a rose.

Right: Discover more about your own nature by gazing into the pure colours of a rainbow bouquet.

THE HISTORY OF HEALING
WITH COLOUR

Ancient cultures worshipped the sun – whence all light, and therefore all colour, comes – and were aware of its healing powers. The therapeutic use of colour in the ancient world can be traced in the teachings attributed to the Egyptian god Thoth, known to the Greeks as Hermes. Following these teachings, Egyptian and Greek physicians – including Hippocrates, the father of Western medicine – used different coloured ointments and salves as remedies, and practised in treatment rooms painted in healing shades. In 1st-century Rome, the physician Aulus Cornelius Celsus wrote about the therapeutic use of colour, but with the coming of Christianity such ancient wisdoms came to be associated with pagan beliefs and were disallowed by the church.

The Arab physician Avicenna systematized the teachings of Hippocrates in the 9th century. He wrote about colour both as a symptom of disease and as treatment, suggesting, for example, that red would act as a stimulant on blood flow while yellow could reduce pain and inflammation.

Scientists and philosophers of the 18th century were concerned with the material world,

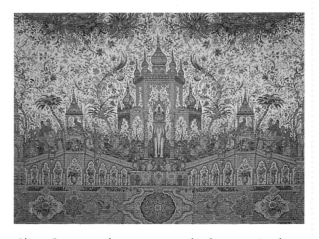

Above: In many cultures, orange and red are associated with physical energy, creativity and life.

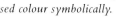

Left: Medieval manuscripts used colour symbolically.

and insisted on visible proof of scientific theories. Medicine focused on cures for physical ailments with advances in surgery and drugs, and less quantifiable healing techniques that dealt with spiritual and mental well-being were rejected.

Colour therapy re-emerged at the end of the 19th century. Edwin Babbitt, who published *The Principles of Light and Colour* in 1878, achieved world renown with his comprehensive theory, prescribing specific colours for a range of conditions.

Despite the medical establishment's continued scepticism, therapists in this century have developed the use of colour in psychological testing and

Above: The Egyptians believed that the colour red had its strongest influence in the afternoon, and in the autumn.

physical diagnosis. The Lüscher Colour Test was based on the theory that colours stimulate different parts of the autonomic nervous system, affecting metabolic rate and glandular secretions, and studies in the 1950s showed that yellow and red light raised blood pressure while blue light tended to lower it.

The use of blue light to treat neonatal jaundice is now common practice, and it has also been effective as pain relief in cases of rheumatoid arthritis.

LIGHT WAVES AND COLOUR

Light is a small portion of the electromagnetic spectrum, which also includes X-rays, ultraviolet and infrared light, microwaves and radio waves. The wave is the characteristic movement of all these types of energy, just like the waves on a body of water. Electromagnetic waves always travel in a straight line as they radiate out in all directions from their source.

The distance between two crests of a wave (the wavelength) determines which type of wave it is. Some wave-crests are over a metre apart – these are television and radio waves. Others are very close together – only billionths of a metre apart. These are gamma and cosmic rays. Around the middle of the spectrum is the tiny portion we experience as visible light.

Left: Most of today's understanding of colour has its roots in the work of Sir Isaac Newton.

Within the visible spectrum, further gradations of wave-spacing produce different colours. The longest waves are at the red end of the spectrum, and the shortest at the purple end, with the other colours falling in between in order of their wavelengths. These pure colours are often referred to as "rays" by colour therapists. Just off either end of the spectrum visible to us are infrared and ultraviolet light, which are perceptible by other creatures such as snakes and honey bees.

Life on our planet has evolved to be able to perceive this narrow range of wavelengths. Other parts of the spectrum with long wavelengths (such as microwaves) or short wavelengths (such as X-rays) actually destroy living things. The sun, our local source of almost all of the electromagnetic spectrum, emits plenty of these long and short waves, but we are protected from them because our atmosphere screens them out at present – when we damage the atmosphere with pollution, we are ultimately harming ourselves.

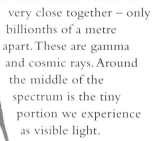

Left: A white beam shot through a prism registers all the colours of the electro-magnetic spectrum, from red to purple.

Right: The colour spectrum is the visible part of the electromagnetic spectrum.

THE PSYCHOLOGY OF COLOUR

THE HUMAN BODY is intimately keyed to colour through its very evolution, and colour therapy is an important method of treatment. Colour affects your personality, whether because of cultural conditioning or your initial experience of a particular colour. If you have experienced a happy event in the past when you were wearing the colour blue, for example, it may remind you of special happenings.

We are influenced by the distinctive vibrations that each colour possesses. Each colour in the spectrum vibrates at its own rate and these vibrations correspond with the body's inner vibrations. Each part of the body resonates to a different colour. When we are ill or troubled we can use the appropriate colour to harmonize our vibrations and restore equilibrium.

There are psychological associations with each colour, and colours can be linked with moods. Reds, oranges and yellows are warm and expansive and give a feeling of energy, excitement and joy. Blues, indigos and purples are calming and cooler. They quieten the temperament and induce relaxation. The psychology of colour is a language that you can learn, in the same way that you learn the alphabet in order to read and write. When you understand its basic meanings you can interpret what it reveals.

When you are well you may like most colours, but emotional and physical problems will tend to bring out preferences for different colours. Often you will be drawn to the colour you need, such as vigorous reds when you are exhausted. You will be naturally attracted to blues when you need some rest and healing. The over-excited would benefit from blues, but depression needs yellows and golds. This basic guide to colour will help you to check specifically what is happening in your system, and to choose the pertinent colour to correct the situation.

Left: The colour energy of crystals has enormous potential for healing.

Right: The human psyche is wrapped in the colours of the rainbow.

BRILLIANCE: THE RAY OF RAYS

Brilliance brings all rays of colour into perfect balance. Many people mistake brilliance for white, but brilliance is the light from which all colours spring. Brilliance is the clear light at the end of the tunnel that people recall after near-death experiences.

Brilliance itself is not a colour: it is the original or cosmic light. Brilliance represents the universal intelligence. It has the purity of the trinity of love, power and wisdom. Our local source of brilliance is the sun.

Without brilliance there can be no vision. Brilliance cuts directly through to the truth. It is the hard light that exposes all flaws and corruption. It contains the essence of all qualities, both

Left: The transparent diamond in its clear brilliance sparkles with every colour of the rainbow.

positive and negative, sparkling in the brilliance of perfection. It clears the way for necessary actions. Brilliance clears any cloudiness in a person or colour. To recharge yourself at any time simply visualize pure brilliant light. When we say that someone is "brilliant", we are really acknowledging his or her purity of vision and action.

Above: Brilliance makes all things grow. It is a state of perfection that exists within the cosmos.

Left: A burst of the sun's brilliance does wonders for the body and mind.

BRILLIANCE AND PARTS OF THE BODY

Brilliance relates to the lymphatic system, and the tissues that filter out the debris from the body.

USING BRILLIANCE

Brilliance brings a ray of hope to your life when all seems lost. Brilliance brings change, whether you like it or not. It allows the delusions of your life to dissolve. Situations become clearer; you

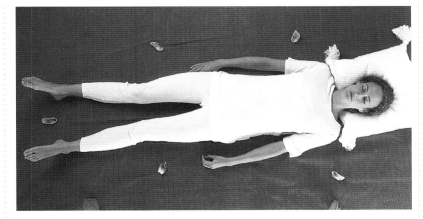

can wipe the slate clean and start again. It may bring about a move to a new home, a change of job, or a subtle inner transformation so that people recognize a new you. Old patterns fall away to be replaced with joy and an uplifting of the spirit.

Add a touch of brilliance to any colour and it will become brighter. Water is liquid brilliance: bathing in a waterfall is the equivalent of standing under a cascade of clear light. Or expose yourself to clear brilliance by taking a brief sunshine bath: you can renew yourself again and again.

Above: This star-shaped placement of clear crystals around the body, known as the Seal of Solomon, increases clarity and quietens the mind, allowing brilliant insights to come into your consciousness.

Below: Brilliance captured in clear crystals encapsulates order, purity and clear thinking.

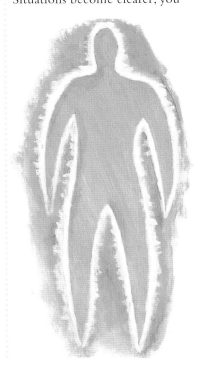

Left: The glow of brilliance surrounds the whole body.

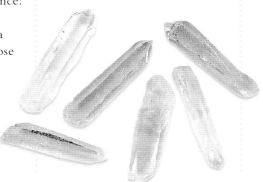

RED

Red is the spirit of physical life, full of power, fire and drive. It is courage and liberation, passion and excitement. Red has a burning desire to get somewhere, but tends to act without thinking. Red people are reformers and fighters, and at best are fine leaders. They are builders of great things from very little. They are explorers, with the energy of the life-force at their command. Pioneers – military and entrepreneurial – relate to red.

At its best, red will ensure a satisfying and passionate love life. Red at its worst is a tyrant or a brutal murderer, seeking advancement no matter who or what suffers.

Left: Proclaim your heart's desire with red roses.

Right: Red foods act as a pick-me-up, restoring zest, energy and drive.

RED AND PARTS OF THE BODY

Red is associated primarily with the genitals and reproductive organs. The red glands are the gonads and the ovaries. Another area of red focus is the blood and circulation.

CAUTION
Do not use red lighting (chromotherapy) above the waist for heart conditions. Medical advice should be taken for any heart problem.

Red prompts the release of adrenalin into the bloodstream – hence its connection with aggression and fear. Problems that respond to red include a clogged circulation or irregularities in the blood supply, hardening of the arteries, infertility, exhaustion and anaemia.

USING RED

Red is a fiery force. It eliminates the unwanted and negativity. Red encourages the shy person to come out of themselves. It puts your life back into action. Red eases

stiff muscles and joints, especially in the legs and feet. It is useful in cases of paralysis, especially when combined with physiotherapy (physical therapy). It acts as a tonic for anyone who catches colds or chills easily, and is good for a sluggish circulation.

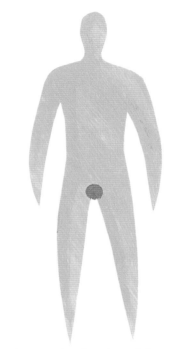

Above: Red is the colour of the sexual organs.

Above: Wear bright red nail varnish or lipstick for sexual power.

RED OPPOSITES
Expansion – Devastation

POSITIVE RED
KEYWORDS
Chief • Resolute • Fighting •
Vigorous • Diligent •
Appreciative • Reviving

NEGATIVE RED
KEYWORDS
Brutal • Lecherous •
Prejudiced • Harsh •
Bullying • Obstinate •
Dishonourable

Left: For an exciting day, let your child wear red.

ORANGE

Orange is self-reliance and practical knowledge. In its role of assimilator, orange is the intestinal laboratory. It tests, then accepts or rejects. It has impetus, and is extremely persistent. But where red bullies, orange bides its time. Orange is genial, optimistic, tolerant, benign, warm-hearted. It is friendship, the life and soul of the party. The unkind practical joker is the negative orange.

Orange shatters; it breaks down barriers. Orange can eradicate. It brings up the energy of a past event that needs to be assimilated. Orange strength is subtle – it stimulates gently. It broadens life and is very purposeful. Orange moves on: it is the colour of divorce! Orange gives the courage to face the consequences. It accepts what is – and then changes it. Orange will not let sleeping dogs lie. It believes in the community. Orange people are usually skilled cooks or good at sport.

Left: In the flower world, the orange marigold represents the doctor.

Above: Bring changes into your life with the stimulation of orange: try the effect of a tawny hair colour.

Below: This marmalade kitten's nine lives are bound to be lucky ones.

ORANGE OPPOSITES
Action – Indolence

POSITIVE ORANGE KEYWORDS
Lavish • Tender • Unselfish • Liberal • Brave • Genial • Vital

NEGATIVE ORANGE KEYWORDS
Arrogant • Gloomy • Domineering • Free-loading • Deceptive • Vain

ORANGE AND PARTS OF THE BODY
Orange is connected to the lower back and lower intestines, the abdomen and the kidneys. It governs the adrenal glands and our gut instincts.

USING ORANGE
Grief, bereavement and loss respond well to treatment with orange. Orange will bring you through the shock of deep outrage and will give added strength where it is needed to pull through adversity. Orange

Above: Orange governs gut instincts.

Right: Boost your dietary assimilation with a dash of orange.

removes the inhibitions and psychological paralysis that occur when people are afraid of moving forwards.

Asthma, bronchitis, epilepsy, mental disorders, rheumatism, torn ligaments and aching and broken bones all respond to treatment with orange. Orange is also useful in alleviating intestinal cramps.

YELLOW

Yellow is the mind, precise and optimistic, clear and in control through the intellect. It is the colour of the scientist. It unravels and reveals, leaving no stone unturned. It focuses attention, loves new ideas and is flexible and adaptable. Yellow has no hesitation; it decides quickly and acts immediately.

Yellow smartens the reflexes. It is the great communicator: the journalist, the entertainer. It has no shortage of words. Yellow unifies and connects – a favourite pastime is networking. When something is revealed to yellow it immediately thinks of editing it for the public rather than feeling it for itself.

Yellow is financial ambition – holding on to it may be more difficult.

Left: Yellow clothes make you quick, alert and daring.

Left: Bask in the yellow sunset to help get your priorities right.

YELLOW OPPOSITES
Alertness – Evasion

POSITIVE YELLOW
KEYWORDS
Fresh • Unprejudiced •
Incisive • Fair • Speedy •
Sharp • Honest

NEGATIVE YELLOW
KEYWORDS
Cynical • Faithless •
Preoccupied • Superficial •
Hasty • Critical • Imprecise

It is at the executive level of business and has the ability to get things done. Yellow despises pettiness. It has self-control, style and sophistication.

Yellow always broadcasts a feeling of well-being. People feel good around those under the yellow ray. They are sunny and willing, unless they are upset, when they can become acid and sharp-tongued.

Yellow is connected to the seat of self-confidence and self-esteem in the body. There is no fat on yellow – it is so quick that excess has no time to gather.

YELLOW AND PARTS OF THE BODY

Yellow is connected to the pancreas, solar plexus, liver, gall bladder, spleen, digestive system, middle stomach, the skin and the nervous system.

Below: Yellow governs our stomach.

Left: Yellow foods bring in the sunshine, releasing depression.

Above: Sunflower yellow represents mental rigour and precise, clear thoughts.

USING YELLOW

Physically, yellow gets rid of toxins and stimulates the flow of gastric juices. Mentally, it clears away confusion and negative thinking. Emotionally, it boosts low self-esteem, lifts depression, and is particularly useful for fears and phobias.

Yellow is also good for menopausal flushes, menstrual difficulties and other hormonal problems. It sometimes helps to relieve the symptoms associated with diabetes, rheumatism and anorexia nervosa.

GREEN

Green is harmony; it stabilizes. It is midway between red and purple: green is the bridge, the gateway in the spectrum – as the heart is in the body. The lesson of love needs to be learnt in order to cross green's bridge.

Green is idealistic, socially aware, helpful and selfless. Doctors and nurses are on the green ray. It is dependable and diplomatic. Green can see both sides but can be moralistic.

Green is clarity and understanding. It helps you to

GREEN OPPOSITES
Stable - Unstable

POSITIVE GREEN
KEYWORDS
Discreet • Sensible •
Fruitful • Benevolent •
Tolerant • Talented

NEGATIVE GREEN
KEYWORDS
Suspicious • Bitter •
Unmindful • Greedy •
Bland • Undependable •
Disappointed

Above: A walk in green fields will renew your connection with nature and restore your inner balance and harmony.

Right: Healing herbs incorporate the power of the colour green.

do the best you can. Green is about finding one's niche. It is self-acceptance.

Green is prosperous, especially in business. Green is the "good life" and the love of collecting possessions. It is wanting the best. Positive green is the giver. It is

88

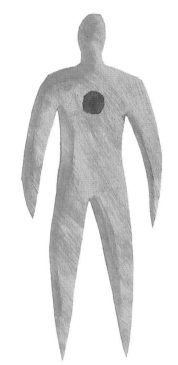

Above: Green governs the heart.

generous and loves to share what it accumulates. It is a love of working outdoors.

Green can indicate difficulty in finding a settled way of life. There may be a conflict of ideas and emotions that causes commotion and upheaval. But with green's ability to discriminate and balance, this conflict can lead to correct judgement and action.

GREEN AND PARTS OF THE BODY

Green is connected to the thymus gland, heart, shoulders and chest, and the lower lungs.

USING GREEN

Green is made up of two primary colours: yellow and blue. Yellow brings clarity and blue brings insight. In combination, these two primaries aid memory. This makes green an important healing colour because most of our physical and mental illnesses result from events in the past.

Use green as a tonic. It is good for shock and fatigue. It helps biliousness, soothes headaches and is beneficial in cases of claustrophobia. It restores stability to anything malignant.

Below: Green foods encourage detoxification and enhance physical stamina.

BLUE

Blue is the spirit of truth and the higher order of intelligence. The head and the heart speak directly through the blue throat.

Blue brings rest; it cools and calms; it slows down, and even retards growth. Blue is the tranquil spirit, the colour of contemplation. Its thinking is

Below: Surround yourself with relaxing blues in the home.

Above: Blue flowers will help you to get into a contemplative mood.

quiet and discriminating. "Still waters run deep" is a blue motto. Blue is peace with a purpose. It values integrity, honour and sincerity. Blue has a poised quality and will not easily draw attention to itself.

Although honesty is a blue keyword, its negative side is a master of manipulation, so skilled

Below: Use blue stones to promote a tranquil spirit.

that you do not even know you have been manipulated. Blue does not like upsets or arguments – yet it often causes them. Blue always advises caution. It is highly inventive. Poetry, philosophy and writing are all blue professions.

BLUE AND PARTS OF THE BODY

Blue is the throat area, upper lungs and arms, and the base of the skull; it relates to weight gain. The connected glands are the thyroid and parathyroids.

Right: Blue governs our throat and our expression.

USING BLUE

Because blue governs the throat, infections in this area are psychologically related to not speaking out. The blue personality hates arguments and often resorts to coughing and spluttering to avoid confrontation. The colour blue will help clear this by counteracting the deep internal

Above: Blue foods promote tranquillity for jaded constitutions.

terror of letting it all "spill out". A stiff neck, often representing the fear of moving forwards, can benefit from the application of blue. Children's ailments, such as teething, ear, throat and vocal problems can be treated with blue. It can also be used for incontinence.

Use a blue light bulb to flood the sickroom with blue light – it cools and calms. It is particularly useful in reducing fevers, and for the terminally ill.

INDIGO

Indigo has force and power. It transmutes and purifies. It unravels the unknown; it can see more than is apparent.

There is no in-between for indigo: it is all or nothing. Indigo is very conscious of the rungs of the ladder. To be out of step is a fate worse than death for indigo.

Indigo aspires to be a spiritual master: it is the inspired preacher and writer. Indigo can reconcile science and religion. But blind devotion is an indigo failing. Negative indigo is the believer who has become a fanatic. All addictions relate to negative indigo. Indigo knows when to move and when to hold fast. It constantly pushes you into reviewing your life. As structure is an indigo aspect, it promotes justice and peace. Lawyers and actors relate to indigo.

Left: Gaze into the indigo of the midnight sky to prepare yourself for the next step in your life.

Below: Meditate with indigo candles to transmute and purify your life.

Above: Indigo represents the skeleton.

INDIGO AND PARTS OF THE BODY

Indigo represents our bone structure, especially the backbone, and also the pituitary gland, the lower brain, eyes and sinuses.

USING INDIGO

Indigo is the strongest painkiller in the spectrum. It can clear up bacteria and the results of air, water and food pollution.

Indigo is good for acute sinus problems, which psychologically are often uncried tears from childhood. Use it for chest complaints, bronchitis, asthma, and for the treatment of lumbago and sciatica, migraine, eczema and inflammations. It helps to bring down high blood pressure and is particularly effective for an over-active thyroid. It is helpful in the control of diarrhoea and is the best antidote for insomnia. It aids kidney complaints and disperses growths, tumours and lumps of any kind. Emotionally, it can help to cure deep hurt.

INDIGO OPPOSITES
Devout – Faithless

POSITIVE INDIGO
KEYWORDS
Discerning • Organized •
Optimistic • Tenacious •
Pure • Compliant

NEGATIVE INDIGO
KEYWORDS
Immoderate • Authoritarian •
Submissive • Puritanical •
Obsessed • False

Above: Put some structure back into your life with indigo foods and experience its steadfast energy.

Below: Hold an indigo crystal to unravel the unknown.

PURPLE

Purple is the royal ray, the ruler, the spiritual master. It is also the protector and the spirit of mercy. Purple is the aristocracy of the spirit; it strives for enlightened perfection. Purple is the visionary; it works with the highest levels of thought, seeing and hearing without using the physical senses. Purple uses its psychic perception on an everyday basis.

Above: Amethyst is the great protector. Look out on a lavender field to feel its comforting cloak of security.

Left: Place purple flowers near you when you are working, to relieve eyestrain.

CAUTION
Purple light should never be directed on to the face, but applied only to the back of the head.

Purple comes to understand that the price it must pay for its royal attributes is sacrifice. Humility is a key aspect. But it can sacrifice itself for the benefit of all without being a victim or a martyr. Negative purple can be belligerent and treacherous.

Purple is the great teacher who realizes that the pupil has to understand – facts alone are not

Below: Purple represents the brain.

> **PURPLE OPPOSITES**
> Serenity – Hostility
>
> **POSITIVE PURPLE KEYWORDS**
> Magisterial • Altruistic • Noble • Personal • Artistic • Boundless • Mystic
>
> **NEGATIVE PURPLE KEYWORDS**
> Merciless • Spiritually haughty • Self-important • Depraved • Snobbish • Dictatorial

enough. Clergymen, musicians and painters all work with the colour purple.

PURPLE AND PARTS OF THE BODY

Physically, purple represents the top of the head – the crown, the brain and the scalp – as well as the pineal gland.

USING PURPLE

Purple is a colour to be used sparingly. It is a "heavy" colour, and long exposures to purple may be depressing. It can reveal deep-rooted depression and even suicidal tendencies.

Right: Purple foods will help put you in the right mood to face conflicts in your life.

It is a useful colour, good for any kind of internal inflammation and for subduing palpitations of the heart. Purple is a good colour for head problems or any irritation of the scalp. The immune system and jangled nerves can also benefit from purple. It is not recommended for use with children, whether in clothing or lighting: if it is used with children, exposure times should be kept very short or it could be introduced in lighter shades first.

Should you suffer from an overload of purple, the antidote is exposure to gold – gold lighting, decor or clothes.

BLACK

Black is the colour of the person who keeps control by not giving information to others. Black indicates that something is lying dormant or buried. It is connected to philosophical thoughts and ideals.

Someone wearing black continuously may be saying that there is something absent from his or her life. Negative black believes that all is ended, there is nothing to look forward to. It is afraid of what is coming next.

Left: Dressing in black says: "I'm young, I'm ready and I'm totally in control."

Right: Wearing black jewellery will announce "I have hidden potential."

But at the heart of black is discipline: this brings about freedom, which is wonderfully liberating. Any cause that gives genuine support and works toward the light is working with the magic of black. Black can complete the incomplete. The mystic arts relate to black.

BLACK AND PARTS OF THE BODY
There are no parts of the body specifically connected to black except when seen on X-rays or in the aura as disease.

USING BLACK
Use black in a positive way to encourage self-discipline. To break the stagnation of black, introduce colours. Encourage the person to reach out.

Left: A black feather represents respect for the old.

BLACK OPPOSITES
Abundance – Nothingness

POSITIVE BLACK KEYWORDS
Beneficially strong •
Creative • Idealistic •
Secretly wealthy

NEGATIVE BLACK KEYWORDS
Destructively strong •
Troublesome • Superior •
Despairing • Constrained

Below: Black foods heighten your awareness of the magic within you.

96

WHITE

White is next to the cosmic intelligence of brilliance, a denser brilliance. White has just stepped down from the ultimate purity of brilliance. Its fundamental quality is that all colours are equal in white. White has supreme faith, which it derives from reason. It conjures up hope, but on the negative side white is its own worst enemy.

Below: Bridal white symbolizes purity in the human form.

Above: Gazing into white clouds creates simplicity and a wonderful feeling of transcendental perfection.

White travels light, so it's drawn to professions that are streamlined and precise. The civil service, banking and ergonomics suit it well.

WHITE AND PARTS OF THE BODY
The eyeball is connected to white: its shades of whiteness are used in diagnosis.

USING WHITE
As white contains equal amounts of all the colours, it does not distinguish one organ from another. Wear it as a tonic to top up the colours in your body's system.

WHITE OPPOSITES
Unspoiled – Dirty

POSITIVE WHITE KEYWORDS
Unsullied • Comprehensive • Benevolent • Truthful • Concordant

NEGATIVE WHITE KEYWORDS
Secluded • Barren • Harsh • Rigid • Unsuccessful

Below: White foods help to clear the lymphatic system of debris.

GOLD

Gold is purity. Gold means "I am". It does not seek, it has already found. It is the soul's experience of all that is past. Gold has access to knowledge and – most important – to knowledge of the self. It is forgiveness and letting go of the past out of a deeper understanding. It expands the power of love because it trusts completely.

Negative gold will blow its own trumpet. Gold's conceit is that of privilege and belief in itself as inherently more worthy than others.

True gold is a belief in honour among men. Gold is extremely gracious. It has the gift to release, but it knows what is needed. Gold is related to the wise old sage.

Below: Golden foods symbolize trust, which allows success to follow.

Above: Golden berries and leaves have the fruitfulness of maturity.

GOLD AND PARTS OF THE BODY
No parts of the body connect with gold, an offshoot of yellow. It can be seen in auras, however.

USING GOLD
Gold is very beneficial for both physical and psychological depressions – it is uplifting. It dissipates suicidal tendencies. It is good for any kind of digestive irregularity, irritable bowel syndrome, rheumatism and an underactive thyroid. Gold is beneficial for the treatment of scars and scar tissue.

Right: Gold jewellery represents the well-heeled; it is naturally associated with money and wealth.

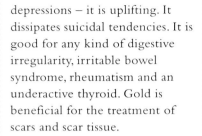

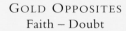

GOLD OPPOSITES
Faith – Doubt

POSITIVE GOLD
KEYWORDS
Mature • Enlightened •
Abundant • Lenient •
Achieving

NEGATIVE GOLD
KEYWORDS
Cynical • Mistrusting •
Obstructive • Sullen •
Misfitting

SILVER

Silver is the thread of cosmic intelligence. An invisible silver cord is said to attach us to "the other side". It stills the emotions and is the great natural emotional tranquillizer. Silver illuminates and pierces; it lights up the path. It penetrates and lays bare. The silvered mirror reflects: it can reveal that a person is full of illusion and living a life that doesn't exist.

Negative silver shows up in relationships in which there is no substance, just delusion. People who fall in love with stars of the

Below: Surround a favourite image with the endurance of a silver-coloured frame.

SILVER OPPOSITES
Increasing – Decreasing

POSITIVE SILVER KEYWORDS
Revealing • Contemplative • Impartial • Astute • Flowing

NEGATIVE SILVER KEYWORDS
Deceitful • Disconnected • Slippery • Inauthentic

silver screen are under the negative of silver. Professions that create make-believe work under silver's influence.

Silver resolves disputes. It takes an unbiased stand.

SILVER AND PARTS OF THE BODY
There are no body parts specifically connected to silver. The feminine dimension of the self is silver, whether it resides in a male or female body.

Right: Use silver cutlery for an important lunch to ensure unbiased discussions.

Above: The silvery moon has the two faces of sadness and romance. It is also the greatest natural tranquillizer – it stills the emotions.

USING SILVER
Silver is good for calming the nerves as well as the hormones. It harmonizes and brings about a fluid state of consciousness. Bathe in the moonlight to restore your equilibrium.

TURQUOISE

Turquoise is single-minded and looks to itself first. It is the colour that says: "Stand still! What do I think? What do I need?" Turquoise says what it feels rather than what is appropriate. Its basic motivation in life is personal relationships. Negative turquoise can be deceived about itself. It

Left: A turquoise silk scarf will allow you to speak out in your relationships.

Above: The stillness of a turquoise stone calms the panic that follows emotional shock.

can be an emotional manipulator.

The antique business is well suited to turquoise, as is working with animals. Turquoise is good at sharing as it hates to be alone. It just loves family life.

Below: Turquoise jewellery is the greatest healer for affairs of the heart.

TURQUOISE AND PARTS OF THE BODY

Turquoise is connected to the throat and chest.

USING TURQUOISE

Turquoise feeds the central nervous system and soothes the throat and chest. Turquoise also encourages self-questioning and coming to know what you want. It helps you to get on with life. Turquoise can help to dispel emotional shock.

Below: Step into a turquoise sea to restore peace within yourself.

TURQUOISE OPPOSITES
Autonomy – Egotism

POSITIVE TURQUOISE KEYWORDS
Calm • Introspective • Self-reliant • Self-possessed

NEGATIVE TURQUOISE KEYWORDS
Reserved • Indecisive • Undependable • Boastful • Narcissistic

GREY

Grey is the bridge between black and white, where innocence and ignorance meet. Grey at its best is optimistic, and knows that the best is yet to come. At its weakest, it believes it cannot have it today. It might get it tomorrow… but tomorrow never comes.

Negative grey is conventional to the point of narrow-mindedness. It is the shade of suffering and poverty.

Grey offers a helping hand. It helps one break free the chains that bind. Grey usually does the jobs that no one else wants to do.

GREY OPPOSITES
Black - White

POSITIVE GREY KEYWORDS
Well-versed • Sane • Authentic • Reputable • Spartan

NEGATIVE GREY KEYWORDS
Destitute • Carping • Dispirited • Ill • Miserable • Depressed

Above: The bright grey of pewter opens one up to receive grace and understanding.

GREY AND PARTS OF THE BODY
There are no body parts connected specifically to grey, but when grey appears it represents breakdown.

USING GREY
Grey is not commonly used in healing, but light grey is extremely soothing. It can help to

Above: Slate-grey is the colour of austerity. There is a belief in grey that there is never going to be enough.

Above: Grey can be divine in its destruction, because it makes way for renewal.

restore sanity. When the skin and nails have a grey tint, it is an indicator of congestion somewhere in the body.

Below: Grey chains represent persistence and endurance.

SHADES AND TINTS

When we talk about colour we usually refer to the hue, which indicates a single colour such as green, blue or red. However, each colour has many facets, and appears in many different guises.

Colours may be experienced as light or dark, bright or dull; touches of other colours in the spectrum result in many variations of tone within each colour.

Below: All tints have a proportion of white in them, and all shades have black.

Below: Pink is constant affection, loving and forgiving.

All tones of a colour share that colour's underlying qualities, but their psychological meanings are modified according to whether they are a higher (tint) or lower (shade) tone of the colour. For instance, scarlet, crimson and flame are the most active of the reds. Reds with a touch of brown – russet and maroon – are more subdued and cautious in character. Pinks, which are tints of red, are much lighter and gentler than the basic colour.

Colour therapists work with the seven colours of the spectrum together with their shades and tints.

Right: Emerald green is connected to wealth and abundance.

Right: Pale blue is the soul searching for maturity.

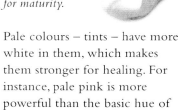

Pale colours – tints – have more white in them, which makes them stronger for healing. For instance, pale pink is more powerful than the basic hue of red because of the abundance of white it contains. Shades of a colour are darker, with the basic hue mixed with black.

Generally speaking, the tints of any colour are considered positive and the shades negative. But the negative can be useful too, because it can alert us to problems that we may need to identify and address.

RED

MAROON: Subdued and cautious; deeply thoughtful; overcomes adversity.

MAGENTA: Spiritually uplifting; the great improver and arbiter.

CRIMSON: Does not believe in strife; strong but kind; tenacity and freedom.

Above: The shade violet is always striving for spiritual awareness.

SCARLET: Love of life; willingness.
PINK: Comforting and mollifying; ripeness; affection.

ORANGE

DARK ORANGE: Undermining; the gambler; the loser.
AMBER: Gives confidence and supports self-confidence.
PEACH: Helps communication; impeccable behaviour.

YELLOW

DARK YELLOW: Low self-esteem; gloomy; the grumbler.
LEMON YELLOW: Orderly; brittle; the misfit; astute.
CITRINE YELLOW: Capricious; superficial.

PRIMROSE YELLOW: Supersensitive; searching.
CREAM: Expansion of space; reassurance; slackness.

GREEN

DARK GREEN: Possessiveness; blindness to another's needs; remorse or resentment.
OLIVE GREEN: Self-deception; bitterness; endurance; mercy.
EMERALD GREEN: Material affluence; easy-going nature; abundance.
JADE GREEN: Generosity of spirit; balanced, natural wisdom.
PALE GREEN: Fresh starts; immaturity; inability to make up one's mind; unhappy childhood.

BLUE

DARK BLUE: Focused; just; a worrier; repressed.
AZURE BLUE: Supreme happiness; contentment with a purpose;

Below: The indigo shade has the power to see what cannot be seen.

Left: Peach, a tint of orange, puts forth the quality of gentle persuasion.

release from bondage and tyranny.
SKY BLUE: Calm, constant love; ability to overcome all obstacles.
PALE BLUE: Uplifting; ambitious; a giver; determined to succeed.

INDIGO

DARK INDIGO: Always waiting in the wings; the dawn never comes. (Indigo does not have a tint.)

PURPLE

DEEP PURPLE: Arrogance; corrupt power; delusion; ruthlessness.
VIOLET: Adores to revere; a rebuilder of hope; intuition; sense of destiny.
AMETHYST: Mystical connections; idealism; protects the vulnerable.
MAUVE: Makes the right choices; aristocratic; dynastic.
PLUM: Old-fashioned; pompous; full of false pride; boring.
LAVENDER: Perceptive and fragile; elusive; aesthetic.
LILAC: A bright personality; vanity; glamour; romance; adolescence.

HIDDEN COLOURS

When working with colour it is important to be aware of what are termed hidden colours, particularly when using colours for healing. Orange, for instance, is made up of the hidden colours of red and yellow. The eye will see orange but the body will also experience the red and yellow vibrations that are within the orange. Therefore, when working with orange for healing, look for the psychological aspects that relate to red and yellow as well as to orange.

The colour green has its own healing meaning, plus the yellow and blue that make up green. Similarly, purple has red and blue within it, so remember to evaluate these colours also. Grey, of course, consists of the hidden colours black and white.

All these hidden colours are important for their psychological meanings and are not to be confused with the pigments artists use for painting.

Above: Blue and yellow are the hidden colours in green.

Above: Yellow and red are the hidden colours in orange.

Below: Green, yellow and blue are the hidden colours in turquoise.

COMPLEMENTARY COLOURS

Every colour of the spectrum has an opposite colour that complements it. This is particularly helpful for healing and can be used in everyday life. It enables you to pinpoint instantly the appropriate colour for support and help.

For example, if you feel extremely irritable and furious at someone's behaviour, at that moment you will be reacting to an overload of red vibration within your system. To counteract this, just think of blue, put on some blue clothing or gaze at a blue object. Continue to do this until you

Right: Red is the colour of efficiency and activity, while blue calms and stills the mind and body.

Above: Orange and indigo support each other when used for healing.

feel the anger pass. Or you may find yourself in a room with yellow decor that you find disturbing. Rather than leave, close your eyes and conjure up the colour purple, the complementary of yellow, to dispel the vibration of the yellow.

The complementary colour of red is blue, that of orange is indigo and yellow's is purple. Green, the middle colour of the

rainbow, has magenta, which is made up of red and blue, as its complementary. This index can also be of use when you are using a lamp with coloured slides for healing. For instance, use a blue slide to relieve the red of irritability, or vice versa – use a red slide to pull you out of the blues you find yourself in.

If you are ever in doubt about a colour, or have a feeling that too much colour has been used, just flood yourself with green – if you are using a lamp – or visualize it. Green acts as a neutralizer, returning balance and order to any situation.

Below: Use green to balance an overabundance of white.

COLOUR CONSCIOUSNESS

IT HAS BEEN OBSERVED that the absence of light can cause a person to suffer both in body and mind. So it is important when creating a home environment that you take into consideration the sunlight that penetrates your rooms. Exposing the occupants to as much sunlight as possible increases their chances of remaining healthy. Although it is unwise to sit exposed to the direct rays of the sun unprotected, it is important that the glow from the sun's beams is received into your psyche. As a radical figure in the development of health care, Florence Nightingale was well aware of the purifying effect of sunlight. Allowing sunlight to flood into dark corners rids any room of its staleness and kills some bacteria. It also lifts the spirits. We reach out towards the light and withdraw from its absence.

Colour is a sensation. It enriches the world and our understanding of it, and we use it as a code. A knight of old would give his lady his personal colours to wear before he went into battle. Colour helps us to determine when fruit and vegetables are ripe. Our skin changes colour with shock, shyness or excitement. Too much yellow light can cause arguments between people, and blue light can quieten them. Colour enriches our lives, whether it is red for danger and green for go, a purple and gold sunset, or a beautiful rainbow.

Colour leads into all realms of life on earth and in the universe. There is a mystery about colour that bewitches us. It is there for us to use, and there is no better way to use it than by harnessing its strength and benefits to enhance our homes and environment.

Left: Relaxing in a green bathroom will soothe headaches and act as a general tonic to help you forget the stresses and strains of the day.

Right: The good use of hot colours in a room instils cheerfulness and stimulates the senses.

USING INTERIOR DECOR EFFECTIVELY

The physical and psychological effects of colour should be taken into consideration whenever you are decorating your home or office. You can use colour in these areas for therapeutic reasons as well as just visual enjoyment. Blending colours successfully can help to alleviate depression, nervous breakdowns and aggression. In fact, all mental, emotional and physical problems can be alleviated if you understand the language of colour.

When you are deciding how to decorate a room it is important to think about the effects the colours you use will have on its occupants. Consider how the room will be used, but also the people who will use it: do they have any problems that could be

alleviated or worsened by your colour choices? What are their ambitions and aims?

Don't forget the furniture, flooring and fabrics that are to be used, and the practicalities of making any colour changes: it is far easier to change the colour of a wall than it is to replace a fitted carpet or expensive furniture.

Take into consideration the size and shape of each room: the stronger the colour, the smaller a room will seem. Small rooms tend to look more spacious decorated in single pale colours. Colours become more intense in larger areas than in small ones, and a strong colour can enclose a room, causing claustrophobia. Dark narrow rooms need light, clear

Below: Paint your china to introduce beneficial colours to your dining room.

Below: Yellow decor in a kitchen inspires efficiency, with no time wasted.

Above: Use gold accessories in the dining room for a feeling of well-being among your guests.

colours. You can also alter the apparent shape of a room by the correct use of colour, for example, a darker ceiling shortens high walls, whereas painting the ceiling in a paler colour than the walls opens up a room wonderfully.

Check how much daylight the space gets before using white, as it can be tiring for the eyes and cause frustration. Dark colours in a room may look good with the sun on them, but will become several shades duller at night in artificial light. If you are painting only one wall in a different colour, do not choose a wall where there is a door or window as this dissipates the colour energy.

HOW TO ENHANCE THE MOOD OF YOUR HOME

The colours of your home should be well balanced to suit your needs or purposes, and to minimize stressful problems.

ENTRANCE HALL

A hallway can have a warm, strong colour that is welcoming, such as coral pink, peach or gold. Green in the hall would suggest to guests that you are hospitable and welcoming hosts.

Below: The complementary colours of red and blue create a harmony in this hall space.

LIVING ROOM

Yellow promotes a feeling of well-being and will put people in a good humour. Brown can give a sense of security. Beige goes anywhere, but you need to introduce one or two stronger colours with it.

DINING ROOM

Orange in a room helps to overcome shyness, but red and orange will make you eat more quickly. Green will help to counteract an overload of red.

KITCHEN

A blue kitchen is inclined to slow you down just when you need to be chopping and peeling energetically. Yellow decor in a kitchen inspires efficiency, with no time wasted.

BEDROOM

Red in a bedroom tends to stimulate too much and cause sleeplessness; indigo would be a better colour to use to avoid insomnia. Indigo in the bedroom is also a useful colour if you suffer from headaches.

BATHROOM

Turquoise is a good colour to choose for your bathroom, where it will feed the nervous system. Add a touch of blue for calmness. Add plants and seashells around the bath, with rich dark green candles for detoxification.

Above: The earthy brown chair and wooden floor will encourage the sitter to develop their full potential.

Right: This blue and white combination helps relaxation and promotes a feeling of safety.

Below: Adding the colour red to a kitchen will stimulate action and speed up efficiency.

HOW TO ENHANCE THE MOOD OF YOUR OFFICE

A few decades ago, coloured decor for offices was almost unthinkable. Drab browns, grey and dark green were the norm. Today, the trend is to make the most of the effect that colour has on people and the advantages this can create. Promoting the effective use of colour in the office is important both for the comfort of the employees and the productivity of the business. Improperly applied, colour can interfere and distract from work, but it is best to avoid white offices. Brown creates tiredness and non-production; grey induces depression and melancholy; black restricts movement and keeps everything on hold.

Above: Blue in the study area will bring a sense of calm and promote inspiration for the writer.

Below: Incorporate red in your office equipment to boost zest, energy and drive.

If you use beige, add green or rose to alleviate the negative slackness that too much beige can bring.

Don't forget details like stationery, as they also make a colour statement. You could even consider changing from the standard white, which can cause distraction from the written word. Refer to the psychological meanings of colours to choose the appropriate one for your company's image.

THE CITY OFFICE

Offices in which activity is high, in areas such as sales and banking, should use red upholstery. This definitely puts workers in the hot seat and adds

Above: Green can be useful in the office when your main aim is to bring abundance and money.

impetus and drive to their performance. Add green walls to counteract the red and reduce headaches that are brought on by the pressure of work.

THE EXECUTIVE OFFICE

When you are the boss you need an office where employees and directors can talk to you and at the same time be reminded that you lead the way. A rich purple carpet gives an impression of big ideas and creativity along with luxury. Gold decor encourages trust and loyalty, but don't forget to add green plants to represent money and balance.

THE OPEN-PLAN OFFICE

For a large office that is partitioned, you would be well advised to make the overall decor a basic cream and introduce bright colours for the paintwork. Use orange, emerald green, rose and rich blue. If only one colour can be used, choose a bright turquoise as this will enable people to feel a little privacy.

THE HOME OFFICE

An office at home can encourage the workaholic. An effective combination would be a royal blue carpet with yellow curtains and pale blue or primrose yellow walls: this should succeed in keeping the business in the office only, and not allow the work to penetrate into your personal life.

THE WHITE ROOM

It became very fashionable a few years ago to have totally white decor in a room: white carpet, sofa, walls – in fact, the whole apartment was turned over to pristine white. The promotion of white interiors had more to do with enhancing the careers of decorators and designers than with benefiting the occupants.

An overload of perfectionist white, if you are surrounded by it for too long, will cause agitation and frustration. Too much of any colour has its side effects. So it is with white decor. Placing one red object in the room, or arranging flowers of the same hue, will dissipate the barren sterility that too much white can cause.

Below: Look at all the coloured gels before deciding which colour is right for the way you feel now.

The all-white tradition in hospitals could do with a little breaking up by the introduction of other colours. Lavender would be a good idea for post-operation recovery rooms, blue would help to calm fear and pre-operative nerves, while peach and pink would introduce a little stimulation when it's time to get patients up on their feet again. You can help friends and relatives staying in hospital by taking in appropriately coloured flowers.

The benefit of an all-white room in your own home is that it offers, at the flick of a switch, the perfect healing sanctuary. By installing a lighting system that enables you to turn on any colour at will, you can flood the room with your chosen colour. This enables you to be bathed in a colour treatment for maximum health and well-being. Imagine returning home after a hard day's work in need of some rejuvenation. All you have to do is turn on the red light and sit in the room swamped with a rich, red vibration for 10 minutes.

You can also achieve this effect by acquiring a free-standing spotlight and selecting a coloured slide or gel appropriate to your needs. Place the gel over the spotlight, taking care to ensure it is not touching the hot bulb. Turn off any other lights in the room and turn on the spotlight. Sit in the path of the spotlight's ray and bathe in the coloured light for an instantly available, on-the-spot therapy.

Right: Bathe yourself in the green vibration to bring in positive thoughts and creativity.

HEALING WITH COLOUR

DISEASE IS REGARDED AS an enemy, but it is possible to think of it as your best friend. It is telling you the truth about yourself, and the ways in which you are out of harmony with the "real" you.

There are several ways of harnessing the vibration of colour for health and well-being. Colour does more than just please the eye. You can eat it, drink it, wear appropriately coloured clothes or jewellery, absorb the colour through your skin or eyes, or decorate and light your home specifically with colour in mind.

Wholesome, fresh food will be full of colour energy. Become aware of the different colours of foods you choose, as your preferences can convey valuable information about yourself via the meanings

Left: Contemplate with yellow to release yourself from exhaustion and depletion.

Right: Learn to colour yourself healthy, wealthy and wise.

Right: Focus on a crystal to centre yourself, and to receive divine healing.

of your chosen colours.

Your home can be a haven of health when you decorate and furnish it in the appropriate colours. House plants are a must. An extremely therapeutic way of working with the colour green, which acts as a tonic for the body, is to do some gardening, or walk in the country under the trees or over the grass. The vibration of brown earth will bring to the fore your full potential, particularly when you are turning the earth over and planting.

Working with colour and understanding the connection between yourself and colour offers a key to good health and vitality.

NOTE
Colour healing can be combined in a complementary way with other therapies. It should not be used as a replacement for medical treatment.

Mood Foods

Different coloured foods can be taken in by the body to heal and stimulate health. Eating the appropriate coloured foods can help to rejuvenate and balance the system.

Seek out foods that are organically grown with no additives, as this will keep the colour vibration alive. Processed and junk foods are dead foods. Microwaving food removes its colour energy, and will create internal disharmony.

Red, orange and yellow foods are always hot and stimulating. Green food can be used to balance the body and is a tonic for the system. Blue, indigo and purple foods are soothing and cooling.

Below: Red foods promote tireless energy and lively action.

Above: Green foods help prevent self-depletion.

Below: Enjoy a rainbow fruit salad to alleviate colour starvation.

Food Colours
RED: Gives extra energy • Heals lethargy and tiredness
ORANGE: Creates optimism and change • Heals grief and disappointment
YELLOW: Encourages laughter, joy and fun • Heals depression
GREEN: Improves physical stamina • Heals panic, fear and apprehension
BLUE: Brings peace and relaxation • Helps concentration • Heals anxiety
INDIGO: Puts back structure into life • Heals insecurity
PURPLE: Promotes leadership • Heals and calms the emotionally erratic

COLOURS FOR DIETING

Right: To encourage weight loss, stimulate your system with the colour yellow. Orange will help the body absorb nutrients from the food.

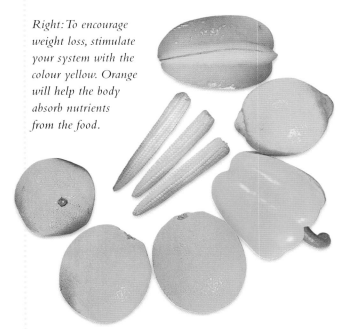

If you are following a sensible diet designed to help you lose or gain weight, the appropriate colour can be used as an aid.

WEIGHT LOSS: YELLOW

To eliminate excess body fat, the colour to use is yellow. Wear it, eat it and drink it. Alternatively, use the Coloured Blooms of Knowledge meditation, visualizing a rich yellow bloom. Psychologically, the colour yellow does not want to carry excess baggage, hence its use in losing weight. Yellow is the nimblest colour of the spectrum and promotes energy and agility of both mind and body. Wear yellow when you exercise and it will keep you moving and pepped up.

WEIGHT GAIN: BLUE

To encourage weight gain, steer yourself towards blue. Wear it, eat it, drink it and visualize it. Blue curbs activity, which allows the calories to gather and turn to flesh. Psychologically, blue does everything quietly and with discretion. It will not be rushed, creating the right emotional environment that is needed if your body is to be given a chance to increase itself. Blue calms the nerves and the glandular system which encourages the curves.

Left: To encourage weight gain, steer yourself towards the blues.

119

CHROMOTHERAPY

Left: A moderate amount of sunlight can be used as a cleanser.

The concept of chromotherapy, or light treatment, is not new. The effect of colour and coloured light has been applied through the ages, from ancient Egyptian temples to the stained glass windows of medieval churches that saturated the congregation with light. Nowadays, paediatricians prescribe a three-day course of blue light for the treatment of jaundice in newborn babies, while modern surgical techniques use laser beams in place of scalpels. Sunlight itself can be used as a cleanser, killing harmful bacteria. Containing all the colours of the spectrum in equal amounts, sunlight is an important nutrient and is vital to our well-being.

The principle involved in chromotherapy is simple. By using different coloured gels or slides in front of high-powered lamps, you can bathe the body or pinpoint a specific problem area with any colour you require for healing. The application of different coloured lights directed on to the physical form can bring about relief both for the body and the spirit. The recipient of the treatment can either lie down or sit in a chair, with the lamp directed towards them. If in any doubt, and for serious illness, consult a medical practitioner.

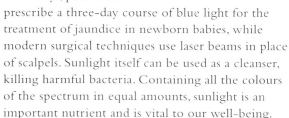

Left: Sunlight through stained glass is a wonderful way to receive coloured light.

Right: Chromotherapy can be used on specific areas: here, the elbow is pinpointed with healing orange to help release stiff ligaments.

COLOUR HEALING AIDS

The therapeutic power of colour can be applied using a variety of other aids and tools. Check the colour profiles for guidance on the colours to use.

CRYSTALS

Gaze at crystals of many colours, until you become aware of which one beckons to you. The colour connection will give you a key to issues that need addressing. Use the appropriate colour for any ailment, such as blue crystals for a sore throat, or a rose quartz if you need a little comfort or love. Just pop it into your pocket so that you can carry it around. Touch it occasionally, feeling its vibration.

COLOURED CARDS

Colour a set of white cards, shuffle them and set out three cards every day. The first one shows the morning's prospects; the second one lunchtime and the third card represents activities later in the day. If your last card is contractive blue or indigo, you certainly won't be going out that night.

Below: Wrap yourself in pure colour vibration with turquoise silk to calm the central nervous system.

CLOTHES

Clothes can be worn to boost any form of healing or to enhance a mood. The skin absorbs very little colour vibration from the material, but psychologically the colour has a profound effect on the person wearing the clothes and also on other people. If you need to wear a colour that you can't stand, then introduce it as underwear in a paler tint, such as peach instead of orange. When colour is paler, the body can absorb it more easily.

By wrapping coloured silk around your body, you can envelope yourself in pure colour vibration. Even a small, green silk square placed behind your head in a chair can relieve tension and pressure.

TORCHES, WATER AND SALT

A torch can be used to beam the appropriate colour on to a pressure point while it is being stimulated. Colouring a Jacuzzi bath, with its underwater lighting, is a wonderful way of combining water with colour vibration. Salt colour-rubs can be used to help invigorate paralysed limbs. Fill a linen bag with sea salt and impregnate it with colour from a spotlight. Then gently massage it over the body.

MEDITATION: CELESTIAL HEALING RAYS

Meditating allows you to focus on yourself and gather all those scattered energies. This process, engaging colour as a healing agent, can be performed at any time and anywhere that suits you. You can play forest music if you wish.

1 Close your eyes and envision yourself sitting in a green meadow with a cool, crystal-clear stream running by you, with fragrant flowers all around. The day is clear and bright, with a soft breeze gently swirling around you. The sky is blue, with a scattering of soft, white clouds.

2 Choose a colour that you need for your personal healing and well-being.

Below: Let the seven colours of the spectrum be your colour guide in meditation.

3 Choose one of the clouds in the sky above you. Let this special cloud become filled with your chosen colour and start to shimmer with its coloured, sparkling light.

4 Allow the cloud to float over you; as it does, it will release its coloured shower, allowing a sweet, tinted mist to envelop you as it sparkles all around you. Visualize your chosen colour as stars cascading in all directions.

5 The mist settles on your skin. It gently becomes absorbed through your skin until the colour has entered deep into your very core, completely saturating your system with its healing vibration.

6 Allow the colour to run through your body and bloodstream for at least 3-4 minutes, giving your body a therapeutic rainbow tonic wash.

7 Allow the pores of your skin to open so that the coloured vapour can escape, taking any toxins with it. When the vapour runs clear, you can close your pores.

8 Stay quietly with your cleared, healed body and mind for a few minutes. Take in three deep breaths, releasing each breath gently, before opening your eyes.

Right: Meditate out of doors to connect to your higher spiritual dimension.

MEDITATION: COLOURED BLOOMS OF KNOWLEDGE

Meditation incorporating colour visualization is thinking in pictures as opposed to words. The colour that emerges gives insight into our emotional state. This meditation allows you to ask for answers to questions that need resolving.

1 Find a comfortable resting-place for yourself and close your eyes.

2 Transport yourself in your mind to an exquisite garden, with you sitting on a grassy mound in the middle of it.

3 There are flowers of every kind and colour surrounding you. Take in the heavenly fragrance while choosing a single blossom.

4 Focus in on the colour of the flower. Ask for guidance with your question while drinking in the colour's vibrations.

5 Let your eyes follow down the green stem into the roots in the earth below.

6 Take a deep breath in and exhale; open your eyes. The colour of the chosen bloom is the key to solving your problem. Let your intuition speak to you, and read the psychological profile of your chosen colour for guidance.

Left: Red is a colour to rekindle the spirit of physical life.

MEDITATION: THE GOLDEN CRYSTAL SHOWER

In this meditation the colour gold is used to lift the spirits and encourage the inner light to burn brightly within you.

1 Lying down in a relaxed position, take a deep breath in, and on exhaling imagine yourself lying on a floating sunbed on the ocean or a pool, gently moving with the rhythm of the water.

2 The sky is pale blue and across it is an arch of pure gold. Focus on this shimmering band of sun-gold.

3 After a few moments allow the arch to vibrate gently so that cascades of sparkling golden crystals start to float gently towards you.

4 As they touch your body the crystals turn to golden dew drops that are absorbed by your skin.

5 Feel an internal warmth deep inside you as the golden hue surges around your body, creating a wonderful glow.

6 Take a deep breath in and on exhaling open your eyes. Your mind and body have now been recharged and revitalized.

Right: Create a breakthrough in your understanding with a burst of sun-gold.

INTUITING COLOUR

Colour is part of your psychic make-up, as inherent as your sight or sense of smell. Psychic ability is a sensitivity we all have to a certain degree – the ability to fine-tune the senses.

The best way to achieve it is simply to make yourself available and clear of mind, so that which is always there can be picked up. It helps to use a colour tool such as a crystal to connect you to the psychic space. Acquiring glimpses into the unseen can give information regarding unanswered questions. Tapping into the intuitive side of yourself means you have access to the whole.

Below: A simple process using candlelight will enable you to connect to your psychic ability.

A SIMPLE CANDLELIGHT PROCESS

It is not surprising that mystics are often depicted gazing out towards the light. Without light there is no life. Colour is born from light and as such it can be your guide to infinite truth. To begin using light to develop your psychic sense, focus on the flame of a candle. The candle represents the light force and reminds us that we also glow eternally, as the flame does. This simple candlelight process will enable you to gain access to your psychic colour keys.

1 Light a white candle in a darkened room. Sit directly in front of it.

2 Take a deep breath in and relax, allowing your eyes to focus on the gently flickering flame. Remain in this position for 15 minutes, breathing gently.

3 Close your eyes and you will see colours coming from the dark. Stay with this psychic show of colours until no more appear, or until a bland dullness is present. Remember the colours.

4 Open your eyes, take a deep breath in and exhale. Write down the colour or sequence of colours as they appeared. Practise until you can harness the light easily. The colour parade shown to you will give you answers through your psychic sense.

Right: Saturate yourself in the calming blue ray to reach a state of peace and tranquility.

INTUITING COLOUR USING A PENDULUM

Another way to access your intuition is to use a pendulum. A clear crystal one is preferable, but a clear glass bead or button dangling at the end of a piece of chain can do the job quite well.

Begin by tying the crystal or button to the end of a chain or a length of white thread. Hold the other end of the chain between the first finger and thumb so that the crystal hangs down. Place the crystal over the outstretched palm of the other hand and ask the pendulum a question. If it swings round in a circle to the right the answer is "yes". Swinging to the left it is a "no". When the pendulum swings backwards and forwards it is an indication that there is no conclusion.

Right: Use a pendulum with the colour wheel to materialize information from the unseen.

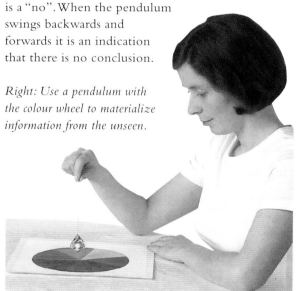

You can use crystals or buttons of different colours for different questions. For instance, if you are seeking information regarding affairs of the heart, use turquoise; for business and finance, use a green crystal.

THE COLOUR WHEEL

Using a large circle of white paper, divide the circle into as many pie-piece wedges as you wish. In each section put a basic colour with its tint and shade: for example red, pink and maroon. You can incorporate as many colours as you wish or fill the whole circle with many shades and tints of one colour only. Hold your pendulum in the centre of the wheel and ask a question. Allow the pendulum to move to whichever section of the board it wants to go to. The colour section it swings towards gives you psychic colour clues to the information you desire. Refer to the psychological profile of your chosen colour to analyse the information.

Always remember that any colour intuiting process can only give indications. The art is in the interpretation. Monitor your findings. You will be surprised at how many of them materialize.

Right: Transform the rainbow into a colour wheel on paper as a tool to help you gain spiritual insight. Use this page, or create your own wheel including shades and tints of each colour.

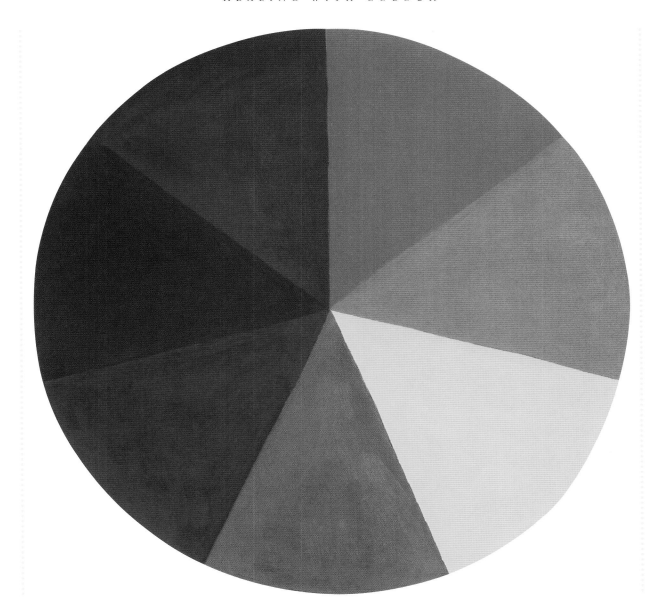

CRYSTAL HEALING

Crystals have long been admired and desired as objects of great beauty. The uniqueness of their structure and the clarity and purity of their form has meant that they have always been associated with healing powers by shamans and healers. Crystals are associated with various qualities, such as the power to calm, energize or soothe. This chapter describes their uses and the way in which they can be used to bring harmony into our lives.

CRYSTAL HEALING PRINCIPLES

CRYSTALS AND GEMSTONES have always been highly prized for their beauty and for their healing and spiritual properties. Costly and difficult to acquire, gemstones have adorned the rich and powerful for thousands of years. Not only is this a display of wealth, it also expresses the hope that the qualities and virtues thought to reside in the stones will "rub off" on their wearers. Healers, shamans and spiritual seekers have been drawn to the clarity and purity of crystals and have made use of their special powers. Crystal healing as it is developing today continues this widespread tradition by exploring new ways in which the mineral kingdom can help restore balance to our lives.

Above: Stability, creativity and clear thinking are associated with crystals that have a warm colour.

Science has yet to discover what is actually occurring during crystal healing, yet this in no way diminishes the real changes that are clearly felt by the participants and the lasting benefits that can be gained. Only by trying out a healing system are we able to judge its worth. This chapter is designed to introduce you to safe and easy techniques so that you can see for yourself why gemstones and crystals continue to play an important role in our lives.

Left and right: Violet stones help the mind to become more organized and orderly.

THE FORMATION, STRUCTURE AND PROPERTIES OF CRYSTALS

Crystals form only in the right circumstances. Deep within the earth's crust superheated gases and mineral-rich solutions at enormously high temperatures sometimes find their way along cracks and fissures towards the surface. As they cool, the constituent atoms, which until now have been randomly agitated, begin to arrange themselves into more stable relationships with their neighbours. This has the effect of building up regular three-dimensional repeating patterns of atoms, known as crystal lattices, in which every atom has found the most stable, balanced arrangement possible.

Crystals continue to grow until all the free atoms are arranged, or until the conditions change. As the solutions cool further and pressure drops, and as different elements join in combination, other sorts of crystals can appear. Usually, harder minerals – for example, diamond, emerald and quartz – will form at a higher temperature and pressure, while softer minerals such as calcite, turquoise and selenite crystallize at much lower temperatures.

A crystal may have remained the same for thousands or even millions of years, or it may have gone through several transformations of shape and form, dissolving and re-crystallizing, being subjected to new mineral solutions or new external conditions that have altered it in some way. (For example, the mineral rhodocrosite can metamorphose from calcite, which looks very different).

All the properties of crystals derive from their unique orderliness and the stability of their atomic structure.

Left and opposite: Crystals form in geometrical shapes according to their component atoms, the outer shape reflecting the inner structure. The cubic system forms crystals that are based on cubes, including fluorite, garnet, copper and iron pyrites.

So the energy and nature of a gemstone is a universal energy, one block in the foundation of life. Biological systems have evolved using the properties and characteristics of a huge range of minerals. When our own energy systems begin to break down under stress the simple, powerful resonance of a crystal may help us to clarify and reinstate our own harmonious patterns of health.

Right: Quartz is one of the commonest minerals on earth and is central to many healing techniques.

Whenever subjected to some outside force, such as heat, pressure, electricity or light, crystals are able to make minute adjustments that quickly restore their internal stability. This is the quality that makes crystals so important in many different areas of technology. We can find crystals used in watches and lasers, and as switching and regulating devices in engines powering everything from cars to space shuttles.

No one knows how crystals and gemstones can help the healing processes of the body. It may be that the nature of crystals spontaneously increases the levels of harmony in their immediate environment. The introduction of a new element of order into a chaotic, disorganized state always tends to increase overall orderliness, because coherence is much the stronger force. Placing crystals, the most orderly matter in the universe, close to an energy imbalance, whether it is physical illness or emotional and mental upset, may encourage our own healing processes to become more effective.

The kingdom of minerals, crystals and rocks constitutes the physical matter of the whole universe.

THE CHAKRA SYSTEM

Knowledge of the chakra system comes from ancient Indian texts. These describe energy centres or chakras in the body, with seven major points arranged along the spinal column. These seven chakras are used in crystal healing.

Chakras are spinning vortices that focus certain frequencies of energy. When a chakra accumulates stress it becomes less able to assimilate and direct the appropriate energy into the body.

Each chakra has a particular focus of action but they are all interrelated. When one chakra becomes disturbed it can upset the functioning of other chakras. Over time this may contribute to physical illness or emotional upset. Depending on your surroundings and activities some chakras may be more active than others. It is best when healing to seek to achieve an overall balance in the chakra system, rather than focusing on only one or two areas.

Each of the chakras is linked with physical functions as well as emotional and mental states, and is also associated with a colour.

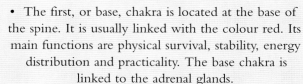

THE SEVEN CHAKRAS

- The first, or base, chakra is located at the base of the spine. It is usually linked with the colour red. Its main functions are physical survival, stability, energy distribution and practicality. The base chakra is linked to the adrenal glands.
- The second, sacral, chakra is situated in the lower abdomen below the navel. Its colour is orange and its functions are creativity, feelings, sexual drive, pleasure and exploration. It is related to the gonads.
- The third chakra is at the solar plexus, just below the ribcage. Its colour is yellow and it is associated with the pancreas and spleen. This chakra identifies and assists in the sense of identity, self-confidence and personal power.
- The fourth chakra is located at the centre of the chest and associated with the heart and thymus gland. Its colour is green and the heart chakra deals with relationships, personal development, direction and sharing.
- The fifth chakra is at the throat, by the thyroid glands. Its colour is blue and its concerns are with all kinds of communication, personal expression and the flow of information.
- The sixth chakra, often called the third eye, is in the centre of the brow. Its colour is indigo and it is linked to the pineal or pituitary glands. It is concerned with understanding, perception, knowledge and mental organization.
- The seventh chakra, the crown, is located just above the top of the head, linked to the pineal or pituitary glands. Its colour is violet and it maintains overall balance of the chakra system and channels universal life energy into the system. It maintains a sense of wholeness and stimulates fine levels of perception, intuition and inspiration.

THE SUBTLE BODIES

Crystals help to regulate the functions of the subtle bodies.

Much of the work of the chakras is concerned with maintaining a healthy balance between the different parts of the individual. The subtle bodies are the energy structures of each aspect of the self which interpenetrate, and extend beyond, the physical body. We are all aware of these non-physical areas of ourselves when we feel our "space" being encroached upon, or when we sense the mood of someone close by. The aura, or auric field, is a general term given to these complex interactions of energy, but they can be differentiated more clearly.

All subtle bodies maintain a flow of information and energy between them. When this flow is disrupted by a stress or trauma it acts like a shadow that blocks vitality to the system as a whole. Placing crystals within the auric field can work on these areas of stagnant energy, releasing them and realigning the whole subtle body system.

THE DIFFERENT BODIES REVEALED

• The etheric body is closest to the physical and provides the blueprint for the body and its organs. A disruption of harmony within the etheric body will almost always precede physical illness.

• The emotional body is the one we feel most clearly from others. It contains the ever-changing patterns of emotion and feelings. Being the least stable of the subtle structures it is the easiest to modify with crystals.

• The mental body contains the patterns in which we have organized our understanding of reality – our beliefs and thought structures – as well as our day-to-day concerns.

• Finer subtle bodies contain our spiritual goals and aspirations, our links to the collective unconscious, and the awareness of larger, universal energy patterns. These can be worked on with crystals, though it is less easy to define these subtle areas of life.

CHOOSING CRYSTALS

This book describes crystals and gemstones that should all be easy to find at reasonable cost. You can start with a very straightforward collection of stones, and the following guidelines suggest a basic working set.

• Small tumbled stones are very useful in crystal healing. For convenience, select stones that will not be too heavy when placed on the body but won't be so small as to get lost easily. Flatter stones will stay in place more easily than round ones. Aim to gather at least two stones of each spectrum colour (they don't have to be the same type of stone).

• Small natural crystals of clear quartz are invaluable. It is useful to have 10–12, each about 2–3cm/¾–1¼in in length.

• Small natural crystals of amethyst, smoky quartz and citrine are less common but well worth acquiring where possible.

• A small hand-sized crystal cluster of clear quartz or amethyst is useful for cleaning and charging your stones and crystal jewellery.

• Larger single stones and tumbled stones are useful to hold and to use as meditation tools. Work with one or two stones that attract you and that you feel happy with. It is better to work well with a few stones, than superficially with many.

Above: Whereas some crystals are hard, others scratch very easily. Even hard crystals may be brittle so store and handle them with care.

Left: Whether a crystal is perfect and clear or battered and grubby it will have the same internal orderliness and potential for healing.

CLEANSING YOUR CRYSTALS

New stones need to be cleansed before you use them. Cleansing crystals removes unwanted energy and restores them to their original clarity, so it should be carried out each time your crystals are used for healing. If you do not cleanse your stones they will become less effective and may pass on imbalances or energetic static. You might detect this as a feeling of heaviness or unpleasantness.

Right: Materials for cleansing crystals.

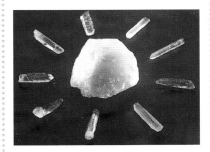

SUN AND WATER
Hold the stones under running water for a minute and then place in the sun to dry.

INCENSE OR SMUDGE STICK
Hold the crystal within the smoke of the incense or smudge stick. Herbs such as sage, cedar, sandalwood and frankincense are used for their purifying qualities.

Placing stones on a crystal cluster will clean them (left); alternatively surround the stone with clear quartz points (above left) for 24 hours.

SOUND
The vibrations of a pure sound can energetically clean a stone. A bell, gong or tuning fork can be used for this purpose.

VISUALIZATION
Take a deep breath and blow over the crystal. Imagine that you are clearing away negativities. Repeat.

SEA SALT
Use dry sea salt in a small container and bury the stone for 24 hours. Don't use salt water as this damages softer stones.

QUARTZ CRYSTALS

Depending on the conditions prevailing during its crystallization, quartz can take on many shapes and sizes. The different shapes can affect the nature of the crystal's energy.

DOUBLE-TERMINATED CRYSTALS have a point at each end. Most quartz grows from a rocky base and forms long, thin crystals with a single point, but if the quartz crystallizes in soft mud or clay it may be able to form points at both ends.

LASER WANDS are crystals that taper towards a very small, faceted point. Usually the sides of the crystal are slightly curved or bent. These stones are ideal for concentrating a tight beam of energy (hence the name), and clearing blocks and stagnant areas.

TABULAR CRYSTALS have two very large flattened faces, as though the crystal has been squashed. This shape increases the speed of energy flowing through it, so these crystals are excellent where extra communication is needed.

GEODES are formed where crystallization occurs in hollow rock chambers originally made by trapped bubbles of air.

HERKIMER DIAMONDS are small, extremely brilliant double-terminated quartz crystals. They are wonderful for energizing and cleansing the aura and are said to enhance dreaming and astral travel if placed under the pillow.

PHANTOM CRYSTALS are so named because within the body of the crystal can be seen smaller outlines of the crystal form. During formation another mineral has begun to crystallize on the surface of the quartz but hasn't inhibited further growth. These are fascinating and beautiful crystals to look at and they make good personal meditation crystals, exemplifying as they do the process of growth and "going within".

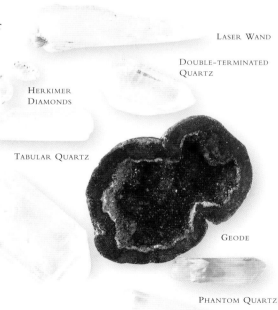

LASER WAND

DOUBLE-TERMINATED QUARTZ

HERKIMER DIAMONDS

TABULAR QUARTZ

GEODE

PHANTOM QUARTZ

DOUBLE-TERMINATED QUARTZ

SHAPED CRYSTALS

Ancient South American ruins have revealed stunning examples of carvings from huge quartz boulders. Today, quartz is carved and polished into many forms, some of which are purely decorative, while others can be of use in crystal healing.

Crystal eggs have always been popular – they are easy to hold and play with, they have stress-reducing comfort and they can also be used as a massage tool directly on the skin.

Crystal spheres have been used for centuries as a means of "scrying", or looking into the unknown, whether at future events or other dimensions. Large crystal balls are rare and expensive, but

small spheres make excellent meditation tools.

Pyramids have a fascination for many and are said to have peculiar energy characteristics. They seem to create large powerful energy fields around them and can be useful for energizing a healing room or other large space.

The obelisk derives from Egyptian sacred architecture and is said to generate an energy field similar to the human aura. In a room, a crystal obelisk creates a powerful focus and balancing effect on the chakras and subtle bodies.

Quartz can be shaped into all sorts of shapes including pyramids, eggs, spheres, obelisks and decorative carvings.

THE QUARTZ FAMILY

Quartz is one of the commonest minerals to be found on the earth and has the greatest number of varieties. It is made up of silicon and oxygen atoms. Some varieties form large clear crystals while others tend to be made up of microscopic crystals packed tightly together in massive form.

Coloured varieties of quartz occur when a few atoms of another element are included within the lattice structure of the quartz molecules, distorting it slightly; or when another mineral crystallizes within the quartz as it grows. Because of their hardness and range of colour these stones are some of those most commonly found in jewellery and crystal healing collections.

TOURMALINE QUARTZ
SMOKY QUARTZ
CLEAR QUARTZ
AVENTURINE
MILKY QUARTZ
CITRINE
ROSE QUARTZ
RUTILATED QUARTZ
AMETHYST

CLEAR QUARTZ is colourless, water-clear and shiny. It may contain cloudy, milky sections or veils that are formed by small bubbles of water or gas trapped within the crystal. Rainbows are created by fractures or complex intergrowths of crystal that greatly enliven the crystal's energy.

AMETHYST is purple or violet in colour. Chevron amethyst has bands of purple and white. It is an excellent general healing stone which calms the mind and is good for meditation.

ROSE QUARTZ is pink and translucent. It rarely forms large crystals. Its energy is gentle but strong and it is a useful balancer of the heart centre and of the emotions.

CITRINE QUARTZ is golden-yellow or orange-brown. It occurs naturally or is made artificially by heating amethyst. Citrine is an energizing stone, physically and mentally.

SMOKY QUARTZ can be pale grey-brown to brownish-black. It is an excellent grounding stone and acts as a deep cleanser.

MILKY QUARTZ is white and contains a high proportion of gas or water bubbles. Its energy is softer and gentler than that of clear quartz.

RUTILATED QUARTZ contains crystals of rutile, looking like golden or yellow strands of hair or sometimes blades of grass. This variety is an excellent healer of torn or broken tissues.

TOURMALINE QUARTZ has embedded within it crystals of tourmaline – usually fine, black needles, but occasionally other colours too. This combination makes it an excellent protecting and strengthening stone.

AVENTURINE is a massive variety of quartz. Usually green but sometimes blue, it can be identified by tiny spangles of shiny silver mica or golden pyrites throughout. Green aventurine is a good heart chakra balancer.

CARNELIAN is a common orange to orange-red translucent quartz that is gently energizing and a useful healing stone.

CHRYSOPRASE forms in bright apple-green masses, a variety of quartz known as chalcedony. It is a relaxation stone.

BLOODSTONE, also called heliotrope, is a dark, shiny green with flecks or patches of bright red jasper. It is gently healing and energizing to the physical body.

JASPER is an opaque quartz of various colours. Most commonly it is brick red, but also yellow, green and blue. It is an all-round protecting and grounding stone.

AGATE is quartz laid down in different parallel, coloured bands, usually wavy or concentric. It comes in all colours though it is sometimes dyed to intensify the colours, especially in decorative slices of stone.

MOSS AGATE, picture agate, tree agate, snakeskin agate and many other types are all named from their colour or from the appearance of inclusions.

JASPER
CHRYSOPRASE
OPAL
CARNELIAN
BLOODSTONE
ONYX
TIGER'S EYE
BANDED AGATE
MOSS AGATE
BLUE LACE AGATE

BLUE LACE AGATE is another variety of agate, named for its delicate blue and white striations.

ONYX is similar to agate but has straight lines of white and black. (Sardonyx has additional brown layers as well.)

TIGER'S EYE is formed where quartz replaces an asbestos mineral to form characteristic plays of light across the fibres of brown, yellow, blue and red. It has an energy that is practical, stable and stimulating.

OPAL is a white crystal which forms in microscopic globules with a high water content, creating a wonderful play of colour. Opal is a stone for working with the emotions.

CRYSTAL HEALING TECHNIQUES: EXPLORING YOUR CRYSTALS

WHEN YOU ACQUIRE A NEW CRYSTAL it is a good idea to spend some time exploring it. This is useful in developing your sensitivity to the subtle energy field.

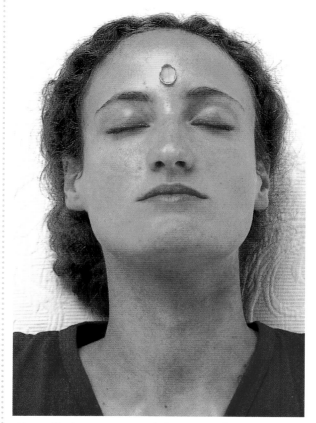

Above: Placing a stone at a chakra point will help you to identify what effects it might have.

1 Look closely at your crystal from as many different angles as possible, then close your eyes and hold it in both hands for a minute or two. Note any impressions or thoughts you may have.

2 Hold the crystal near your solar plexus and, as you breathe out, imagine the breath passing over the end of the stone. Then, on the inbreath, imagine your breath entering through the crystal, directly into the abdomen. Continue this cycle to build up a circuit of energy, then relax.

3 Sit quietly with your eyes closed, then open your eyes and look at the crystal in front of you. Close your eyes after a few minutes and then pick up the crystal. Notice any changes in the way you feel.

4 Hold the stone in your left hand, then put it down and pick it up with your right hand. Repeat several times.

5 Place the crystal on your chakra centres – the most sensitive are usually the solar plexus, heart and brow.

6 Place the crystal close to your body while you are lying down. How does it feel on different sides of the body? Near your head? Near your feet?

A VISUALIZATION EXERCISE TO EXPLORE A CRYSTAL

For this visualization exercise, choose one of your favourite crystals, one you already know quite well.

1 Sit in a relaxed comfortable position, holding the stone in both hands. Take a few moments just to relax and focus on the crystal in your hands.

2 Slowly let your awareness float down into the crystal until you reach a point where you seem to come to rest.

3 In your mind's eye, identify how the crystal feels to you. Is it warm or damp, cool or dry, smooth or rough? Take a minute or two to explore the energy of the crystal through your inner touch.

4 Now relax again and turn your attention to any quality of sound within the crystal, whether it appears to be a tone, a pulse or a tune. Is it high or low? Simple or complex? Listen to the sounds of the crystal for a few moments, then relax again.

5 Take a few deep breaths, then imagine you are breathing in the crystal's energy through your nostrils. What smell, what taste does the crystal have? Can you identify it?

6 Relax once more, then open your inner eyes. Imagine what the structure and the energy of your crystal looks like: the quality of light, the images, the landscapes, scenes and figures that may be related to you. Don't attempt to analyse what you see. Just let the imagery play before your eyes.

7 Now become aware once more of the crystal's taste, its smell, its sounds and its touch. Very gradually bring your awareness out of the crystal and become more aware of your body and the world around you. Take notes so that you remember your experiences.

Right: Hold the crystal near your solar plexus and imagine that your breath is entering your body through the stone.

145

MEDITATING WITH CRYSTALS

Clear quartz has long been used as an aid to meditation and contemplation. Gazing at the water-clear crystal has a very quietening effect on the mind – you are looking into and through solid matter that has extraordinary order and stability. Contemplation of a crystal can help with problem-solving. If you have a particular problem or worry, take a minute or two thinking about the situation and then gaze deeply into the crystal. Don't concern yourself with thoughts: just allow them to come and go. As your mind quietens down you may find a solution, or a new idea may pop into your head later in the day.

Left: Sitting quietly with your crystals will give you greater insight into how they work and how you might use them as healing tools, as well as developing your sensitivity to the energies. Sit comfortably and gaze into a crystal. Take time to look closely at it in detail, then allow your focus to relax. Pay attention to what you may be feeling and the quality of your thoughts. Are they calm or busy? Do they carry a particular emotion, or a certain memory? Notice any sensations in your body. After a minute or so move the crystal away from you and choose another. Repeat the process and compare the experiences. When you have finished, sit for a few moments with your eyes closed and take slow, deep breaths.

Hold a smoky quartz in your left hand and a clear quartz in your right hand. Sit quietly with your eyes closed, or gaze gently into another crystal. After a few moments change the crystals around to the other hand. What differences do you feel? Once you have found a combination that is comfortable and effective spend a few minutes every day sitting with your crystals.

Below: If you find it difficult to settle down quietly with one crystal use your creative playfulness to make a pattern or mandala with your stones. This form of active contemplation can be just as revealing and relaxing as "doing nothing". If you have space, it can be interesting to make a large mandala of stones on the floor and spend a while sitting in the centre.

Above: Place or hold the crystal at a comfortable distance so that you can easily gaze into the depths of the stone. Don't worry about your thoughts or about "doing it right". Just relax and gaze into the stone. After a few minutes, gently close your eyes. If you feel tension or pressure anywhere take a couple of slow, deep breaths and consciously relax again. Repeat the procedure several times if you wish. Take a little time to return to everyday activity when you decide to finish the meditation exercise.

HAND-HELD CRYSTAL HEALING

Whenever we wish someone well there is a natural flow of healing energy. This can be concentrated and enhanced by the use of quartz crystal in combination with directed thought. Here are a few exercises that use simple imagination or visualization skills to direct healing energy where it is needed. A quartz crystal will direct the flow of energy either towards or away from the body, depending on where the point is facing.

An additional stone can be held in the "absorbing" or "receiving" hand. This will help to direct the healing energy very clearly in your mind and, if you choose an appropriate type of stone, the effects will be enhanced. For example, using a rutilated quartz will focus those energies to do with healing tissues and nerves, while a rose quartz will release emotional stress and calm overactivity. A small crystal sphere is a useful shape for the receiving of energies as it stores and passes on energy in a smooth, even way.

Left: If you have an area of over-energy, it can often be identified by a feeling of congestion, heat, pain, tension, irritation, frustration or anger. Place the palm of your left hand over that area. Hold the quartz crystal in your right hand with its point away from you directed towards the ground. As you breathe deeply and evenly, begin to relax and imagine all excess energy releasing from your body and passing out through the crystal into the earth where it can become balanced. Moving the crystal in circles may help you to imagine the process more clearly.

When there is the need to recharge your vitality or if you have some need for extra healing energy, hold the quartz in your right hand pointing in towards the area concerned. Hold your left hand out from your body with the palm facing upwards. As you breathe deeply and evenly, imagine healing energies from the universe passing from your upturned hand through the crystal and into your body.

1 You can also apply the hand-held crystal healing method to another person. To clear away unwanted energy, release tensions and help relaxation, hold your "receiving" hand close to them and with the quartz in your "directing" hand allow the excess to drain away into the earth. You may feel that moving the quartz in small circles helps to speed the process. Try out both clockwise and anticlockwise (counterclockwise) movements.

2 When you finish it is a good idea to recharge the aura with revitalizing energy. So now hold the crystal in the "directing" hand with its point towards the body. Hold your other, "receiving", hand palm upwards and allow universal life energy to flow through the crystal into the newly cleansed area.

Above: Another effective healing method is to sweep a crystal through the subtle bodies. Begin at the feet and slowly move the crystal up the body with increasingly larger circles, always returning to your starting point between the feet. When you have drawn the largest circle reaching to the top of the head, gradually reduce the size of the sweeps and return to your original starting point between the feet, making sure that you focus on that point with a few extra rotations to help "anchor" the energy in a practical way. This is an excellent way to "springclean" someone's aura and remove tensions.

Try these exercises using opposite hands to see how it feels: usually with right-handed people the left hand is more absorbing or "receiving" and the right hand directs the outward flow of energy. If you are left-handed you may find the opposite to be the case.

CRYSTAL PENDULUMS

Right: The correct grip.

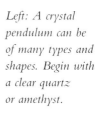

Left: A crystal pendulum can be of many types and shapes. Begin with a clear quartz or amethyst.

Below: If the pendulum goes on moving over an imbalance for a long time without seeming to change, put another crystal on that spot and move on. Check later.

Using a crystal pendulum for healing is effective in removing energy imbalances from the body's finer energy systems.

Have a clear intent that the crystal pendulum will only move away from a neutral swing (back and forth) when it comes across an imbalance that can be corrected quickly and safely. The crystal will move in a pattern that allows the imbalance to be cleared and will then return to the neutral swing.

1 Hold the pendulum lightly and firmly between the thumb and forefinger. Allow the wrist to relax and hold arm and body in a comfortable position.

2 Start the pendulum swinging in a line, to and fro. This is a neutral swing.

3 Slowly move up the centre of the body, beginning beneath the feet. Wherever the pendulum moves away from neutral, simply stay at that point until the neutral swing returns.

4 When you get to a point above the head, go back to the feet and begin again, this time holding the pendulum near one side of the body. Repeat for the other side.

CRYSTAL WANDS

Wands are shaped tools which usually have a faceted point at one end opposite a smooth, rounded base. Sometimes natural single crystals are simply given a rounded base, but most are cut from large blocks. The rounded base allows wands to be used directly on the skin without scratching and they can be a lovely adjunct to massage. They are especially useful to release tension from the head, hands and feet. With a light touch, simply move the wand in small circles over the tense areas. Wands can also be used to massage the subtle bodies.

Below: Crystal wands come in all shapes and sizes and can be cut from a wide variety of materials.

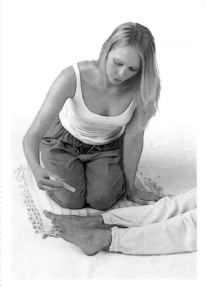

1 Begin at the feet with the wand held point outwards and make small anticlockwise circling movements (which help to release unwanted tensions). Slowly work up the body. You will probably be aware of areas that feel different, where the wand feels heavy, sticky or where you feel instinctively inclined to move in a different way. Allow this to happen and then return to the normal movement.

2 When you reach the top of the head, reverse the wand so that the point faces inwards. Move down the body once again in small circles, but this time clockwise. This recharges the body's energy fields. Once again, you may find that certain areas require greater attention.

ENVIRONMENTAL PLACEMENTS

Crystals can be useful in many different environments. As well as a decorative focus they can help to reduce the effects of electro-magnetic pollution and emotional stress. Crystals adjust imbalances by absorbing excess energy. A crystal securely positioned in a car, for example, can help to reduce tiredness and improve concentration. For clarity, use clear or citrine quartz.

Above: A large piece of rose quartz or amethyst in the bedroom or living room will help to keep the atmosphere light and positive.

Below: We all get difficult telephone calls from time to time. Keeping a small bowl of tumbled stones or a few favourite crystals by the telephone offers a focus for your attention. It will help to prevent unnecessary depletion of energy, or over-involvement in other people's problems, by helping you to keep a balanced perspective during a tricky conversation.

Above: Computers and VDUs, like all electrical equipment, create quite strong electromagnetic fields around them. Putting a cluster of crystal by the computer screen will help to neutralize the harmful effects. You should notice a reduction in fatigue and irritability. Remember to cleanse the crystal frequently.

CREATING A SACRED SPACE

Creating a sacred space allows you to honour those things that are important in your life. It can be as simple as a photograph and a few flowers or as elaborate as a ritual altar. You may like to arrange meaningful objects to make a temporary special display, and this can be a useful contemplative exercise in itself. You can create a sacred space to record or celebrate a special anniversary or event, or you might like to set aside a permanent quiet space where you can take time to be with your own thoughts and memories.

Below: You can make a mini Zen garden by filling a large, flat bowl with clean sand or fine gravel. Arrange interesting stones and crystals to create a miniature landscape. Use an old comb or fork to draw patterns in the sand.

Above: Adding special crystals brings an extra light and beauty to a sacred space, enlivening and keeping the energies fresh and positive.

Above: A quiet corner of a garden makes an excellent place for quiet reflection, and crystals will enhance a mysterious atmosphere as well as helping to keep the plants healthy.

WEARING CRYSTALS

For thousands of years precious and semi-precious stones have been worn as decoration and for their beneficial properties. Wearing crystals is a useful way to help maintain the body's energy levels, but remember the stone can only help you if its own energy is clean. Place your jewellery on a crystal cluster at night to cleanse it, or, if you have had a difficult time, cleanse them with running water or in incense smoke for a minute. If crystal jewellery isn't cleansed regularly, the stones cannot process unbalanced energies and these may even be reflected back into your auric field, making matters worse.

Crystal jewellery is best used when you need a little extra boost. Wear only one or two stones at a time – more may confuse the energy message to the body. Don't become dependent on your crystals; have a couple of days without any from time to time.

Sometimes a stone needs to be somewhere particular on the body. If you don't have a pocket in the appropriate place, use a small bag or pouch and a safety pin to attach it securely to the inside of your clothing.

Left: A simple way of wearing crystals is as a pendant. The length of the chain used will determine which chakra will be most stimulated and balanced. A stone at the solar plexus will influence how you use your store of energy and what you do with personal power; a stone at the heart will affect your emotional state; placed between the heart and throat a crystal will help you define your space and needs; at the throat, a stone will aid your communication and artistic skills.

Crystal earrings can help to balance throat, neck and head energies.

Right: Wearing gemstone rings will stimulate different meridian channels depending on which fingers they are worn on.

MAKING GEM REMEDIES

Gem remedies are vibrational preparations made by placing a sample of a gemstone in a clear glass bowl of pure spring water and exposing it to direct sunlight. Because of the characteristics of water this process allows the energy pattern of the stone to be imprinted on the water. When it is ready the stone is removed and the charged water is bottled and used for helping the healing processes of the body. A certain amount of care needs to be taken with this procedure as some gemstones are toxic or soluble in water. If you would like to try this yourself, gem water is easy to make.

Take a clean crystal of quartz and place it overnight in a glass of water. The charged water can be drunk in the morning. Or keep a water jug (pitcher) with a couple of crystals in it to energize the contents. Use this water to drink or to water plants. Try gem water made from different members of the quartz family: citrine, amethyst or tiger's eye.

USING CRYSTAL LIGHTBOXES

The qualities and properties of gemstones are recognized and valued for the way they reflect, hold and interact with light. A lightbox is a simple device for directing light through a transparent or translucent crystal.

Putting a crystal on a lightbox can create changes of mood and atmosphere in a room. For instance, a red light or a red crystal will be energizing, yellow will increase relaxation, green will have a calming effect, and violet will create mystery.

Right: You will need a stone with a flat base large enough to cover the aperture. If you want to try a clear quartz, those with some milkiness or cloudiness in the base will work best, diffusing the light evenly throughout the crystal. For different moods use coloured lightbulbs or coloured filters to change the colour of light passing though a clear crystal.

A crystal with internal fractures, rainbows or inclusions, such as moss agate or rutilated quartz, will light up magnificently.

TREATING PLANTS AND ANIMALS

You can use the life-enhancing properties of gemstones and crystals to maintain the health of your pets, or to help them through times when they are unwell. There are three main chakra points on four-legged animals: at the top of the head, halfway along the spine, and at the base of the tail.

Using a pendulum or massage wand to balance your pet's energy bodies can be helpful – you will soon know if your pet thinks otherwise! A simple method to give your pet a boost of energy is to add gem water to the animal's drinking water, or you can put a drop or two on your hands and either stroke it on to the fur or sweep it through the auric field from head to tail several times.

Cats are sensitive to subtle energies and they may not appreciate a lot of crystals placed around them. Dogs tend to be less fussy. Any sick animal will appreciate your efforts to help them but watch for any signs of discomfort. A pet that curls up and goes to sleep close to a crystal in its basket has found the

energy comfortable and acceptable. A tiny gemstone can be attached to a dog collar in a small pouch or suspended from the collar by a silver spiral mount.

Left: Crystals in an aquarium show their vivid colours and will energize the surroundings.

Below: Houseplants can also benefit from crystals placed in the top of their pots. Quartz is an excellent stone to use as an overall enhancer of energies. Emerald also has a close affinity with all plants: it needn't be of gem quality – large green beryl crystals are quite easy to acquire. Or you can use aquamarine, a blue variety of the same mineral. Jade is said to amplify the energies of plants and will also help you to attune more closely with them. Turquoise can be used to help plants recover from damage and disease.

CRYSTAL HEALING PLACEMENTS: THE SEAL OF SOLOMON

THE SEAL OF SOLOMON is so-called because a six-pointed star, formed from two interlocking triangles, was often used in medieval magical texts ascribed to King Solomon. The symbol represents the interaction of the four elements and the uniting of heaven and earth. The Seal of Solomon can be used whenever there is a need to relax, physically and mentally. It refreshes the body's energies and clears away stress. It can also be used on a specific part of the body that

CLEAR QUARTZ

needs healing. Depending on where the problem is you may need to have some stones on and some stones off the body. This makes no difference – as long as the stones create the necessary star shape and they remain in the energy field, they will work.

Left: You will need six clear quartz points, which should be placed in a star shape evenly around the body: at head and feet, at shoulder level and knee level. When the points are facing outward there will be a release of any excess energy. When the points face towards the body there will be a charging, energizing effect.

Left: Begin with the points turned outwards for about five minutes, then reverse the stones so that the body is infused with new energy for a minute or two. If you experience any discomfort when the stones are facing in the first direction, try starting with the other placement.

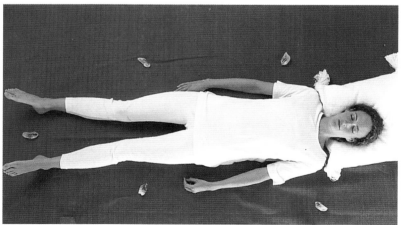

Left: To treat a part of the body, place the six quartz stones around the area with the points facing outwards for a while, then replace the crystals in the same positions, with the points facing inwards. It is sometimes appropriate to place another crystal in the centre of the quartz points to act as a focus for the healing energy.

Below: You can intuitively select a stone for the centre of the star shape, or choose one according to its colour code, using green for calming, for example, activating with red, or cooling with blue. Top row, left to right: jasper will gently ground and energize; malachite will reduce pain. Bottom row: turquoise will calm; citrine will relax; sodalite will cool.

JASPER

MALACHITE

TURQUOISE

CITRINE

SODALITE

GROUNDING AND CENTRING

In order to be effective when using crystals for healing, and in order to gain maximum benefit from crystal healing, you need to be centred and grounded. Grounding is a term that means you are solidly anchored in the present, with a certain inner stillness, a feeling of being secure, in control of yourself and alert. When you lack grounding you will feel nervous, unfocused, and unable to concentrate. When dealing with the energy of crystals and the healing process, being grounded enables you to "earth" excess energy and prevents you from becoming overwhelmed or "spaced-out".

Eating and drinking is an effective way to focus your energies into the physical body: a sip of water or tea and a biscuit is often enough. Chocolate will provide enough sugar-shock to bring you down to earth rapidly!

Physical activity, such as stamping your feet, jumping up and down, doing some gardening or a similar task, are all good grounding exercises.

Above: Holding a grounding stone helps to focus your energy, and such stones are a great help in bringing you back to normal, everyday awareness after a healing session. A simple grounding exercise is to sit or stand with your feet firmly placed on the floor and imagine roots growing from your feet deep into the earth. With each breath, allow the roots to spread deeper and wider until you feel firmly anchored and secure.

Below: For a grounding layout, place a smoky quartz crystal point downwards at the base of the throat and a second smoky quartz between the legs or close to the base of the spine, also with its point towards the feet. This is an excellent way to centre and ground your energies in a couple of minutes. In most crystal healing patterns it is a good idea to use a grounding stone close to the base chakra or between the feet or legs. This ensures that the changes created by the crystals are rooted in the physical body and can be integrated in a practical manner.

Being centred means being physically, emotionally and mentally balanced. You are aware of your own boundaries and in control of your energies. It is a state of calm receptivity in which you can more easily be aware of your intuitive thoughts and subtle feelings. Centring can be achieved by any technique that focuses your attention within your body.

1 Sit quietly and spend a minute simply being aware of each breath as it comes and goes.

2 Imagine you are breathing in from your feet and breathing out through your feet into the earth.

3 Become aware of your midline – an imaginary line extending from above the top of your head to below your feet, situated just in front of your spine. Pull your breath into this midline from above and breathe out through the line into the ground. Repeat until you are calm and focused.

4 Strike a bell, gong or tuning fork and simply listen for as long as the sound remains.

5 Focus your attention on the centre of gravity, located within your pelvic girdle behind and below your navel.

6 Slowly and consciously bring your fingertips together and hold them for a minute or two, breathing deeply. As well as centring this also increases mind/body co-ordination.

Above: Bring your fingertips together slowly to focus your attention.

Below: Some gemstones are particularly effective in helping to ground your energies. Most grounding stones are dark or red, like these pictured below. Top, left to right: snowflake obsidian, haematite, dark tourmaline, smoky quartz, onyx. Bottom, left to right: staurolite, citrine, jasper.

BALANCING AND CALMING CRYSTALS

After a hard day at work it can sometimes take a long time to "wind down" and feel relaxed enough to enjoy your free time. A simple placement of stones can help you to feel calm and refreshed after a couple of minutes.

Below: Clear quartz increases clarity and quietens the mind. Smoky quartz, point downwards, helps release tensions and re-establishes focus in the present. The rose quartz balances the chakra system and the emotions.

ROSE QUARTZ

CLEAR QUARTZ

SMOKY QUARTZ

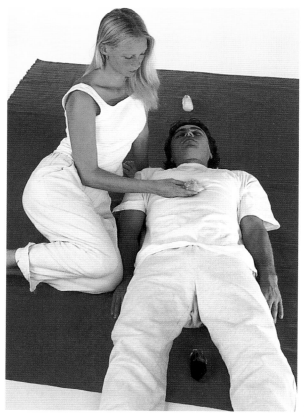

Above: Place a clear quartz crystal, with its point upwards, above the top of the head. Place a smoky quartz crystal, point downwards, close to the base of the spine (between the upper thighs or knees). Put a small rose quartz crystal on the centre of the chest. You should find that four or five minutes is sufficient to feel refreshed.

FEELING "OUT OF SORTS"

Sometimes you may feel as though you are jangled and "not quite right". There is no apparent reason for this sense of disorientation but it is as if you have "got out of bed on the wrong side" that morning. This feeling may wear off during the day, but if it continues try the following placement of crystals.

Below: The stones you will need for alleviating a feeling of disorientation.

Below: Place a clear quartz, point outwards, at the crown of the head. Place a turquoise or lapis lazuli at the centre of the forehead. Finally, place a smoky quartz, point downwards, near the base of the spine.

TURQUOISE

LAPIS LAZULI

CLEAR QUARTZ

SMOKY QUARTZ

CALMING THE HEART AND MIND

There are times when you may feel unhappy or tense because of some stressful situation or when you are unable to do or say what you feel you should. This layout of crystals will help to calm an emotional upset and allow you to focus on the practical solutions to the situation.

Signs of stress being released include fast fluttering of the eyelids; deep breaths or sighs; muscle twitches; yawning; tearfulness, crying and sobbing.

CITRINE

ROSE QUARTZ

CLEAR QUARTZ

AMETHYST

Above: For clearing emotional stress you will need four clear quartz stones together with citrine, rose quartz and an amethyst.

Above: On the centre of the chest, place a small rose quartz surrounded by four clear quartz points. If the points are placed outwards they will help to remove emotional imbalances. If the points are placed inwards they will help to stabilize an over-emotional state. On the lower abdomen, just below the navel, place a citrine quartz with its point directed downwards. This will increase the sense of security and feeling of safety. Place an amethyst on the brow or above the top of the head. This helps to calm the mind. If you feel the release is too strong, remove the stones from the heart area and place a hand over the solar plexus.

ALLEVIATING STRESS AND TRAUMA

A shock, accident or loss may leave you feeling profoundly shaken and insecure. This layout helps you to release stress and gather yourself together again. Look out for the tensing of muscles, mental replays of events and sudden wellings of emotion. Continue regular use of this layout until these signs disappear. This will help to prevent the shock seeping deeply into the system.

Below: For this layout you will need eight small clear quartz crystals, a rose quartz and a tiger's eye.

Below: Place a small rose quartz at the heart centre with four clear quartz points facing outwards, placed diagonally around it. At the sacral centre, below the navel, place a tiger's eye. Surround it with four clear quartz crystals with points inwards, also placed diagonally. The stones at the heart release emotional tension while the stones on the abdomen balance the first, second and third chakras and give stability and grounded energy.

CLEAR QUARTZ

TIGER'S EYE

ROSE QUARTZ

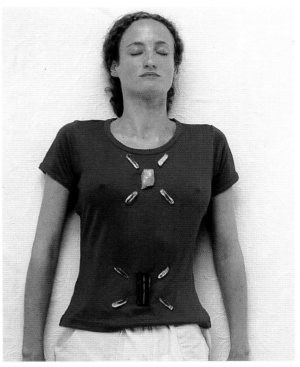

SEVEN COLOUR CHAKRA LAYOUT

One of the simplest ways to help balance the whole chakra system is to place a stone of the appropriate colour on each area. This will give each chakra a boost of its own vibration without altering its energies or the overall harmony of the system. If you lay your collection of stones out so that you can easily see them all you will find your attention goes to the best choice of stone for each chakra. It is a good idea to place a grounding stone, like smoky quartz, between the feet to act as an anchor.

1 Choose a red stone to put near the base of the spine or, alternatively, use two red stones of the same sort and rest one near the top of each leg. This will deal with the base chakra.

2 For the sacral chakra choose an orange coloured stone to put on the lower abdomen.

3 At the solar plexus use a yellow stone, placed between the navel and the ribcage. If there is tension in this area an energy-shifting stone, like a tiger's eye or a small clear quartz point, can be put at the diaphragm to help release.

4 The heart chakra in the centre of the chest can be balanced with a green stone. A pink stone can be added for emotional clearing.

5 For the throat chakra use a light blue stone. Place it at the base of the throat, at the top of the breastbone.

6 An indigo or dark blue stone is normally used to balance the brow chakra in the centre of the forehead. Amethyst or another purple stone can also be used here.

7 The stone for the crown chakra rests just above the top of the head. If you have chosen an amethyst for the brow, use a clear quartz at the crown. If you have used a dark blue stone at the brow you can use a violet stone at the crown.

INTUITIVE HEALING LAYOUTS

You will become more confident at crystal healing when you allow your intuition to guide you to the correct stones and their placement. You will then be able to modify the healing energy to suit different people's needs. "Mistakes" – picking up the "wrong" stone, or putting it in the "wrong" place – are very often an unconscious identification of what is really needed. In order to make appropriate intuitive decisions you need to have a certain understanding of the other person's energy. Begin by using a few simple healing procedures – a balancing layout or a crystal pendulum for example. As you sit watching the other person during the crystal session your attention may go to a particular pattern of stones or an area of the body. This can be an intuitive signal that crystals need to be placed there, or that existing stones need changing in some way. As a practical exercise in developing your intuitive skills try the following healing technique.

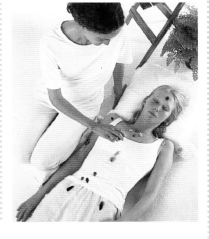

1 Lay all your crystals and gemstones out so that you can see them easily, then spend a minute or two either talking together or use a wand or pendulum to give an initial balance to the auric field. With the person's needs in mind go over to your crystals and pick up those that immediately attract your attention. Don't concern yourself about why you might have chosen them.

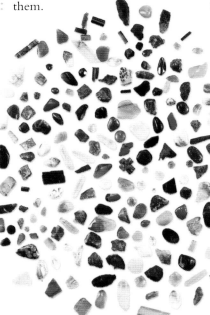

2 Very quickly, without conscious thought, place the stones where you feel they need to be. Don't concern yourself with the placement – they can be anywhere on or around the body. Keep a check on how the person feels and make adjustments where you feel they are necessary. After about five minutes remove the stones and use a grounding stone to settle the energies back to normal. If you like, recheck how the person's energy feels now using a pendulum or wand.

AMETHYST HEALING LAYOUT

Amethyst quartz is one of the most versatile healing stones. This layout can be used in any situation where physical, emotional or mental healing is required. Most people find they can stay comfortably in this layout for up to half an hour. Try to match the size of crystals as closely as possible to give a balanced feel – odd sized stones may give a rolling sensation.

Above: You will need eight amethysts of roughly equal size, evenly spaced around the body. If you have natural crystals place the terminations so that they are facing inwards towards the body. When you have finished you might like to place a grounding stone, such as smoky quartz or black tourmaline, in the centre of the forehead to help you return to the present. Take time before you resume normal activities.

Left: Amethyst is an ideal healing stone. As it balances and quietens the mind you may become aware of an increased imagination and an ability to visualize clearly.

AMETHYST FOR HEADACHES

Amethyst can be very useful in soothing headaches. Headaches tend to occur when there is an imbalance or blockage of energy to the head. This healing pattern helps to free up blocked energies and so reduce the pain.

Right: Place one amethyst point on either side of the base of the neck, just above the collar bones, pointing up towards the top of the head. Place a third stone, also pointing upwards, in the centre of the forehead on the brow chakra. An optional fourth amethyst can be placed, point outwards, at the top of the head.

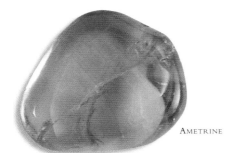

AMETRINE

Above: Another common cause of headaches is an imbalance between head energy and the solar plexus chakra, usually brought about by stress or unsuitable food. If you suspect this to be the case, or if you have a headache with an upset stomach, use a stone that helps to balance the solar plexus – such as citrine or moonstone. In these instances a piece of ametrine, a natural mix of amethyst and citrine – part golden, part violet – is ideal.

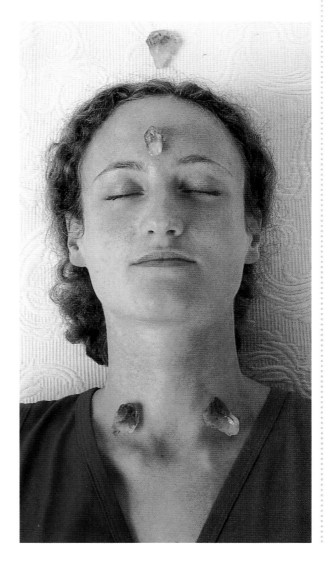

169

EASING PMT AND MENSTRUAL CRAMPS

Period pains and menstrual cramps are often made worse by physical and emotional tension restricting the body's natural energy flows. Moonstone helps to balance and relax emotional states. It also has beneficial effects on all fluid systems in the body and eases tension in the abdominal area.

Below: A healing pattern of five moonstones amplifies the relaxing and healing potential of the stone. Place one moonstone at the top of your head, one on the front of each shoulder by the armpit and one resting on each hip.

DARK OPALS

MOONSTONES

Above: Natural, tumbled and gem polished moonstones. Ancient Indian Ayurvedic texts describe moonstone as the ideal stone for women to wear.

Above: Dark opal has qualities similar to those of moonstone, though it acts more on the first and second chakras where it can often ease menstrual cramps in a very short time. Place a small piece in a hip or trouser pocket. Dark opal is a non-gem variety that can be found in many colours. The most common form is slate grey with an orange translucence.

RELIEVING ACHES AND PAINS

From time to time, everyone suffers from the aches and pains of over-stretched muscles. Sometimes chronic muscle tension can develop from repetitive actions at work, or through maintaining a poor posture at a desk or in the car. Because crystal healing is very relaxing, it will be of general benefit for these sorts of aches and pains. However with really tense, knotted muscles you may need to take a more focused approach.

Above: An effective healing pattern to realign the whole body structure uses eight pieces of dark tourmaline (schorl). First, place four tourmalines in a cross shape: above the head, below the feet, and midway down each side of the body. Each of the remaining four stones is positioned slightly clockwise of the others. This pattern may initially focus your attention on the painful areas – but this soon eases away as the body relaxes and readjusts itself.

Below: Tourmaline, especially the dark varieties of black and dark green (sometimes known as "schorl" and "verdelite"), is excellent for structural adjustment. A painful, knotted muscle can be relieved by keeping a piece of tourmaline near to it. Neck, jaw or head tension can be eased by wearing tourmaline earrings, the long thin crystals making elegant jewellery.

LODESTONE

Above: Lodestone is the traditional name for magnetic iron ore, used for navigation in ancient times. If you place a small piece near the base of the skull and another at the bottom of the spine, back tensions can be helped and the subtle spinal energies stimulated.

Release back tension by placing a small, clear quartz on the centre of the forehead. Imagine a beam of bright white light passing deep into your head with each inhalation.

TOURMALINE

RESTORING PEACEFUL SLEEP

Sleepless nights can be caused by a variety of situations. They can often be overcome by simple strategies – but when you are half-asleep and exhausted, motivation is a difficult thing to summon up. This is when the right sort of crystals can be very useful. Different types of sleeplessness will need different gemstones to ease them, and you will need to experiment – a stone that works for one person may keep someone else awake.

Above: Just hold the appropriate stones or have them nearby. They will help to quieten you so that you can relax and fall asleep.

IRON PYRITES

Above: If your sleep pattern is disturbed by something you have eaten, a digestive calmer like ametrine, moonstone or iron pyrites may help.

STAUROLITE

TOURMALINE

SMOKY QUARTZ

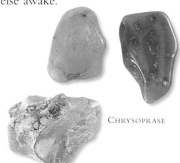

CHRYSOPRASE

Above: Chrysoprase, an apple green variety of chalcedony quartz, has been found in most cases to encourage peaceful sleep. A tumbled stone can be put under your pillow, or a larger piece placed on a bedside table.

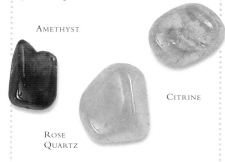

AMETHYST

CITRINE

ROSE QUARTZ

Above: If tension and worry is the cause of restlessness try amethyst, rose quartz or citrine.

Above: Where there is fear, particularly related to bad dreams or nightmares, use a grounding and protecting stone such as tourmaline, staurolite, smoky quartz or tourmaline quartz and place it at the foot of your bed. Labradorite will also help to chase away any unwelcome thoughts and feelings.

RELIEVING PAIN

Pain is the body's way of letting you know that something is wrong and needs attention. Very often pain is caused by an excess of energy of some sort. Using crystals can help reduce pain to manageable levels by releasing blocks within the subtle bodies and stimulating the body's own healing mechanisms. In general, all cool-coloured stones – blue, indigo and violet – will help to calm painful areas and restore the natural flow of energy in a damaged area.

Right: Copper is well-known for its ability to reduce inflammation

COPPER

and swellings of all sorts, and some of the most useful gemstones for controlling pain have high concentrations of copper. Copper itself can be worn as a bracelet or carried in its rough, natural, nugget form to help all energy flow in the body and reduce inflammation.

Above: Malachite is a soft mineral of copper that forms in concentric bands of light and dark green. It is good at calming painful areas and drawing out imbalances. It is a good absorber of negativity and needs regular cleansing to maintain its effectiveness.

Above: Turquoise can be used whenever there is a need for calm healing energy. The colour of the stone stimulates the body's immune system and it has a beneficial effect on many areas.

Right: Carnelian, although it is a warm colour, is a powerful healer of the etheric body and encourages healing.

CARNELIAN

ROSE QUARTZ

Above: Pink stones, such as rose quartz, calm aggravated areas and also reduce the fears that often accompany injury and pain. Placing pink stones at the solar plexus and sacral chakras will calm the mind and relax the body.

MALACHITE

TURQUOISE

ENERGIZING CRYSTALS

A lack of energy is often felt when the body is in a state of imbalance. Correcting the balance using crystal healing techniques will restore your natural vitality. However, when it is needed you can give yourself an extra energy boost by using those stones that directly stimulate vitality.

Below: Red, orange and yellow stones will promote an increase of energy. Bright, strong colours such as a deep red garnet or a golden amber or topaz will be very stimulating and dynamic. More earthy tones – such as tiger's eye, dark citrine and jasper – will tend to focus on an increase in practical motivation. You may find some stones too energizing in certain situations. For example, golden citrine quartz is a wonderful substitute for the sun's warm energy on a dull winter's day, but you might find it uncomfortable in high summer.

CALCITE

RUTILATED QUARTZ

RUBY

AMBER

DARK CITRINE

CARNELIAN

JASPER

CITRINE

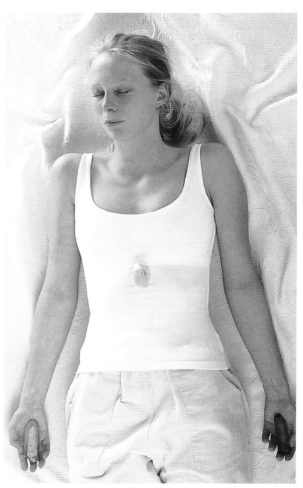

Above: For a quick addition of energy to the whole system hold a clear quartz crystal, point upwards, in each hand and place a large citrine at the solar plexus.

174

AIDING STUDY AND CONCENTRATION

The ability to be effective in learning situations depends upon several factors that can be enhanced by the use of crystals. The mind needs to be clear, focused and alert. Clear quartz brings stillness to the mind, and a grounding stone prevents your mind straying.

Below: Have a favourite quartz crystal near you as you study. Take the stone into a test or examination – it will remind you of what you have learned and will give you extra confidence and clarity.

CITRINE

AMBER

Above: The colour yellow is known to stimulate the logical functions of the mind, so a bright yellow stone like amber, citrine or fluorite will assist memory and recall. Any sort of fluorite is an excellent stone for study as it helps to balance the functioning of the brain hemispheres. This is particularly helpful when you need to do a lot of reading.

KYANITE

SODALITE

SAPPHIRE

Above: Deep blue stones, such as kyanite, sodalite and sapphire, improve communication skills and better understanding of ideas and concepts.

DIRECTORY OF CRYSTALS

Of the many thousands of different minerals on earth, only relatively few are used in crystal healing – mainly those that are abundant and sturdy enough to withstand regular handling. Even so, with all the different varieties and colours available it can be bewildering trying to remember what each stone does and how each can be used. Learning the properties of colour will help you to identify the general functions of a crystal or gemstone.

RED STONES

The colour red stimulates, activates and energizes. It is associated with the first chakra at the base of the spine, which is the centre in the subtle anatomy for action and activity. Ability to use practical skills, movement, motivation, protection, physical survival and the use of life-energy are some of its main functions.

GARNET, in its red varieties, is one of the speediest energizers. It will increase energy wherever it is placed. It will also tend to activate other stones placed nearby.

JASPER, a dark or brick red massive form or quartz, is commonly found on beaches. It is a useful stone to place near the base chakra. It is grounding and gently activating to the functions of the body.

RUBY is a red variety of the very hard mineral, corundum. It works with the energies of the heart centre and the circulation within the subtle anatomies. It is energizing but balancing in its effects.

JASPER

STAR RUBY

JASPER

POLISHED
RUBY CRYSTAL

GARNET
PEBBLE

SECTION OF
RUBY CRYSTAL

GARNET
CRYSTAL

PINK STONES

Pink, a blend of both red and white, has a gentle and subtle way of pushing things towards a resolution. It is related to the actions of the base chakra and the heart chakra, and helps to bring emotions and sensitivity into our daily actions.

ROSE QUARTZ is the best known and favourite of the pink stones. It has a calming and reassuring effect. However, it can also be a powerful releaser of unexpressed emotions where they might be thwarting personal growth.

RHODONITE, when polished, is a salmon pink often flecked with black. This works with the practical aspects of our feelings, and has a greater grounding effect than other pink stones.

KUNZITE is a pale pink and violet stone. Having a striated crystal structure it is an excellent shifter of emotional debris, and also helps self-expression.

RHODOCROSITE is a delicate banded stone of pink, yellow and orange. It will help to improve self-image and self-worth, especially when problems in this area are preventing action. It is excellent for balancing the functions of the second and third chakras.

RHODONITE

ROSE QUARTZ

KUNZITE

RHODOCROSITE

ROSE QUARTZ

ORANGE STONES

Orange is an equal mix of red and yellow, and this combines energizing and focusing qualities. It is associated with the second chakra, which deals with the flow or lack of flow within the body. Creativity and artistic skills are an expression of this flow, while shock, trauma and blocks indicate the lack of flow.

CARNELIAN is the most popular orange stone, characterized by a sense of warmth and a gently energizing effect. It is commonly found on beaches. It will nearly always be of benefit in healing.

ORANGE CALCITE is smooth and lustrous. It is ideal for the delicate encouragement of potential, and because of its softness and watery feel, is good at melting away problems.

DARK CITRINE, orange and browny-orange, is a balanced stimulator that will bring out practical creative skills. It can be used as a gentle grounding and supporting stone.

TOPAZ, with its elongated crystal form and parallel striations running its length, is an excellent clearing stone that can be used to direct energy around the body.

COPPER, which can be found as natural nuggets and crystallized forms, is ideal for use when a lack of flow creates stagnation and clumsiness. It has a beneficial effect on many physical and subtle systems.

TOPAZ

NATIVE COPPER

ORANGE CALCITE

CARNELIAN

CARNELIAN

DARK CITRINE

179

YELLOW STONES

Yellow relates to the solar plexus chakra that regulates the functioning of the nervous system, digestive and immune systems and the ability to discriminate and identify things. Stress, fear, happiness and contentment are all linked to this colour.

AMBER, a fossil tree resin, varies in colour from a lemon yellow to a rich orange brown, including a deep red and green. It has a beneficial effect on the nervous system and self-healing processes.

RUTILATED QUARTZ is a clear or smoky crystal containing fine threads of golden or orange rutile crystals. It is excellent for moving healing energy from place to place, and works well with broken or damaged tissues.

TIGER'S EYE is a variety of quartz with a velvety sheen that looks like a sweet. The packed fibres and the bands of browns, golds and reds speed up energy flow and anchor subtle changes into the physical body.

CITRINE QUARTZ is a popular yellow stone. When it is a bright, clear yellow it will help to keep the mind clear and focused.

IRON PYRITES, known as "fool's gold", helps to cleanse and strengthen. It calms the digestive system.

TIGER'S EYE

CITRINE

AMBER

IRON PYRITES
CRYSTAL

RUTILATED
QUARTZ

TIGER'S EYE

GREEN STONES

Green is found in the middle of the spectrum and it is associated with the heart chakra, located at the midpoint of that system. Emotions and relationships are balanced here and the qualities needed for growth and personal space are encouraged.

PERIDOT

AMAZONITE

GREEN AVENTURINE

BLOODSTONE

EMERALD

BERYL

MOSS AGATE

MALACHITE

GREEN AVENTURINE is an excellent heart balancer. It is gently expansive, allowing for an easy expression of feelings.

MALACHITE will dig out deep feelings, hurts and resentments and will break unwanted ties and patterns of behaviour.

BLOODSTONE is a green quartz with flecks of red jasper, giving it an active balance of energy and calm. It stimulates emotional growth and is of benefit to the heart and circulation.

AMAZONITE calms and balances the emotions and helps throat and lung problems.

MOSS AGATE is ideal for supporting the lungs and easing breathing difficulties, as well as feelings of being emotionally stifled. It brings in the energy of the natural world.

PERIDOT is a vivid light green stone associated with volcanic activity. It is one of the best cleansers of the subtle bodies and will help to motivate growth and necessary change.

EMERALD, the green variety of the mineral beryl, is a help to finding personal direction in activity. It brings clarity and calm to the heart and emotions.

LIGHT BLUE STONES

The throat chakra, associated with communication, works with this colour. Communication using sight, voice, colour, taste, smell – all the senses – is involved at this centre, as are inner forms of communication: the way you talk to yourself, your thoughts and the ability to express yourself all come under the vibration of light blue.

AQUAMARINE, a blue variety of beryl, stimulates the healing properties of the body. It improves confidence and the ability to stand your ground, and helps to release the flow of communication.

TURQUOISE has been used for centuries as a supportive and protective stone. It strengthens all the subtle bodies and the fine communication systems of the body, such as the meridians.

BLUE LACE AGATE is a beautiful, banded variety of quartz that gently cools and calms. It can be used for lightening thought and works well with rose quartz.

CELESTITE is a soft stone that forms clear, delicate blue crystals. Very inspiring and "dreamy" in its qualities, it is ideal for lifting heavy moods and helps with difficulties in expressing spiritual thoughts and needs. It is also helpful for throat problems.

CELESTITE
CRYSTAL

AQUAMARINE
CRYSTAL

TURQUOISE

TURQUOISE

AQUAMARINE

ROUGH
BLUE LACE AGATE

TUMBLED
BLUE LACE AGATE

INDIGO STONES

The brow chakra, the "third eye", is linked to the midnight blue of indigo. Perception, understanding and intuition are qualities of this chakra, together with a deep sense of peace and connection.

LAPIS LAZULI is a rock of different minerals that has a large proportion of deep blue lazurite as well as often being flecked with iron pyrites. It has a powerful effect, stimulating the rapid release of stresses to enable a greater peace to be experienced. Lapis also stimulates the higher faculties of the mind and understanding.

SODALITE can look very similar to lapis lazuli, though it is usually of a less vivid blue and has cloudy veils of white running through it. It calms the mind and allows new information to be received.

KYANITE forms translucent thin blades of crystal that often look like fans. A wonderful mover of energy that is blocked or inflamed, it is calming and clearing and is a rapid restorer of equilibrium to all areas.

AZURITE is most commonly seen as small round nodules but can also forms shiny crystals. It will free up difficult and long-standing blocks in communication and will reveal those structures that are stopping us from using our full potential. It stimulates memory and recall.

SAPPHIRE can be expensive when it possesses the correct depth of colour, otherwise you can find good-sized crystals at a reasonable cost. It relaxes and improves the mind. It balances all aspects of the self by releasing tension and promoting peace of mind.

SODALITE

AZURITE

SAPPHIRE

LAPIS LAZULI

KYANITE

SAPPHIRE CRYSTAL

VIOLET STONES

Violet and purple are linked to the crown chakra located above the top of the head. Inspiration, imagination, empathy and the sense of service to others are the energies of this centre. Violet and purple stones help to rebalance extremes within the systems of the body, so they can be of use when you are not sure of the nature of a problem.

AMETHYST is perhaps the most useful all-purpose healing crystal. It is universally applicable in its uses and benefits. Amethyst is a good stone to use with meditation as it quietens the mind and allows finer perceptions to become clear.

FLUORITE comes in a wide variety of colours, though violet is one of the commonest. It can be used to great effect with the upper chakras where it enables subtle energies to integrate better with normal consciousness, increasing the practical use of ideas and inspirations. Fluorite also helps with co-ordination, both physical and mental.

SUGILITE is a stone with various shades of purple. It can be useful in group situations where it helps to resolve personal difficulties and brings greater group coherence. This stone is also indicated for those who are uncomfortable with their circumstances or who feel as though they don't "fit in".

IOLITE is also called water sapphire, but is no relation. It has a subtle violet translucence that increases the imagination and all aspects of intuitive creativity.

FLUORITE

AMETHYST

SUGILITE

FLUORITE

IOLITE

WHITE STONES

White or clear stones are often used at the crown chakra where they reflect the qualities of universality and clarity of that centre. White light contains within it all other colours, so it symbolizes the potential to reflect all energies. White stones also reflect the energies around them. White is related to the concepts of clarity, cleansing and purification.

CLEAR QUARTZ strengthens and brings coherent energy, as does milky quartz, which has a gentler effect. All the subtle systems of the body are enhanced and clarified. A state of harmony is brought about.

HERKIMER DIAMOND is a clear, bright variety of quartz excellent for all detoxification processes and for cleansing imbalances from the subtle bodies. It will amplify the qualities of the stones placed near to it. Clarity of mind and vivid recall of dream states are commonly induced.

ICELAND SPA is a variety of clear calcite that helps us to relate to the world in a balanced and productive way, with clarity.

MOONSTONE (see p170) is white, milky, creamy or pearly in colour. It has a characteristic soft luminescence from which it gets its name. It is an excellent stone for clearing tensions gently from the emotions and from the abdomen, where it can help the digestive system. Moonstone will work well wherever there is imbalance in the fluid systems of the body.

SELENITE WAND

CLEAR QUARTZ

ICELAND SPA
(OPTICAL CALCITE)

HERKIMER
DIAMOND

SELENITE, also named for its soft moonlight quality, is a type of gypsum. Do not place this stone in damp or wet – the thin slices of crystal will slide apart and disintegrate. Selenite is a good stone for removing emotional turmoil or confusion. It clarifies awareness and helps to reach new states of consciousness.

BLACK STONES

While white stones reflect and clarify light, black stones absorb light. White will reflect the visible, black will show you the hidden potential of any situation. Black is solidifying and manifesting. It holds all energies quietly within itself and so requires patience to explore fully. Black stones are usually grounding, acting as energy anchors to help you return to a normal functioning state. Many will also reveal hidden aspects so that they can be dealt with – in this respect black stones have a purifying role.

SMOKY QUARTZ is a gentle grounding stone. It is protective and is able to dissolve negative states. It will reach to deep levels of the self to cleanse and balance, and so can be a useful meditation stone. Smoky quartz has all the qualities of clear quartz expressed in a steadier, gentler manner.

TOURMALINE comes in all colours but the black variety is called "schorl". It is a good protective stone, grounds energies with great speed, and will help to realign physical problems to do with the skeleton and muscles. As a long thin crystal with parallel striations, schorl is a very good energy shifter.

OBSIDIAN is volcanic glass. It can be pure black or have flecks of white (snowflake obsidian), patches of red (mahogany obsidian) or a smoky translucence (Apache tears). Obsidian is excellent at bringing imbalance to the surface so that other stones can clear it away. It can also be used to find the hidden factors around situations so that the right action can be taken.

HAEMATITE is an iron ore that can be rust red but is more often a silvery grey with a metallic sheen. It will help the assimilation of iron within the body and has a supportive, grounding and centring effect. It is quietening and calming to the mind.

SNOWFLAKE OBSIDIAN

HAEMATITE

BLACK TOURMALINE

SMOKY QUARTZ

OBSIDIAN

MULTICOLOURED STONES

There are many gemstones and minerals in which a mix of colours occurs naturally. You can determine their actions from the colour combinations that they display. In general, stones that display a full spectrum of colour, or that contain rainbow fractures, will be able to reflect a wide range of states and qualities and can therefore be used for a variety of reasons. Stones with a combination of two colours have specific functions determined by those colours.

OPAL is perhaps the best known of the multicoloured stones. With a high water content which refracts light in a multitude of ways, opal works with the emotional balance. Depending on the play of colour, the opal will naturally harmonize with different chakras.

AZURITE-MALACHITE is a mix of these two related minerals. It allows the deepest imbalances to surface and then be removed. It will also help you to express your needs in a clear, direct way.

LABRADORITE appears a dull waxy grey until it catches the light when beautiful iridescent sheets of peacock blues, yellows and oranges appear. Labradorite will deflect any unwanted energies from the aura.

HAWK'S EYE is a blue variety of tiger's eye with gold, green and orange between deep blue strands. It is ideal for the throat, brow and crown chakras, where its rapid energy enhances the flow of information into the body.

AMETRINE is a quartz which shares the colours and qualities of amethyst and citrine, being part violet and part golden. It balances the mind, augmenting the imagination and the rational mind.

LABRADORITE

HAWK'S EYE

AMETRINE

TOURMALINE

AZURITE-MALACHITE

WATERMELON TOURMALINE

OPAL

187

BIRTHSTONES

When you go into a jeweller's or a crystal shop it is likely that you will see stones assigned to each of the astrological signs of the zodiac. The attribution of birthstones has a long tradition and is well worth examining. Most of the lists today, however, have been compiled by the jewellery trade to ensure a good sale of different gemstones throughout the year.

Below: Most stones are associated with astrological signs and planets.

AYURVEDIC SYSTEM

SUN	Ruby, garnet, star ruby, red spinel, red zircon, rose quartz
MOON	Pearl, moonstone, quartz
MERCURY	Emerald, aquamarine, peridot, green zircon
MARS	Coral, carnelian, red jasper
VENUS	Diamond, white sapphire, white zircon
JUPITER	Yellow sapphire, yellow pearl, topaz, citrine
SATURN	Blue sapphire, amethyst, lapis lazuli

THE AYURVEDIC SYSTEM

The oldest known system of correspondence between the planets and gemstones comes from the Indian system of Ayurveda. Here, the positive and negative influence of the planets is assessed and, where necessary, gemstones are suggested to enhance health and success. Large, high quality gemstones are cut and set in the appropriate metals according to carefully laid down procedures and ritual. The individual's circumstances are considered to ensure maximum benefit.

Opposite: The chart shows the Ayurvedic correspondences between planets and gemstones.

TRADITIONAL BIRTHSTONES
The Western system of attributing gemstones to planets and zodiac signs also has a long tradition, beginning in classical Greek and Roman times. Later it was influenced by the Arabs, who knew of the Indian system.

Medieval thought was dominated by the concept of macrocosm and microcosm, where everything reflected the order within the universe. All animals, plants, colours, gemstones and times of day were thought to fall under the "rulership" of a planet.

Our present-day idea of birthstone lists derives from these traditional systems but they should be taken as only a rough guide at best. As individuals with unique patterns of energy and changing needs, it is more appropriate for us to use those crystals that appeal to us, rather than feel we should wear a designated birthstone. This list is a compilation of the stones most frequently associated with each astrological sign.

AQUARIUS	*(20 Jan – 18 Feb)* Garnet, turquoise, amethyst, onyx, ruby, diamond, jade, ulexite, sapphire
PISCES	*(19 Feb – 20 Mar)* Amethyst, turquoise, pearl, rose quartz, calcite, aquamarine, bloodstone
ARIES	*(21 Mar – 20 Apr)* Bloodstone, carnelian, jasper, diamond, aquamarine, emerald, ruby, coral, haematite
TAURUS	*(21 Apr – 20 May)* Rose quartz, emerald, diamond, tourmaline, tiger's eye, topaz, lapis lazuli
GEMINI	*(21 May – 20 Jun)* Citrine, tiger's eye, pearl, moonstone, agate, emerald, aquamarine, calcite
CANCER	*(21 Jun – 20 Jul)* Emerald, chrysoprase, pearl, ruby, moonstone, amber
LEO	*(21 Jul – 21 Aug)* Clear quartz, onyx, turquoise, ruby, topaz, sunstone, emerald, cat's eye
VIRGO	*(22 Aug – 22 Sept)* Carnelian, moonstone, sapphire, opal, peridot, sodalite, rutile quartz
LIBRA	*(23 Sept – 22 Oct)* Peridot, topaz, opal, lapis lazuli, aventurine, emerald, jade
SCORPIO	*(23 Oct – 22 Nov)* Aquamarine, dark opal, turquoise, obsidian, smoky quartz, herkimer diamond
SAGITTARIUS	*(23 Nov – 20 Dec)* Topaz, turquoise, garnet, amethyst, malachite, flint, blue lace agate
CAPRICORN	*(21 Dec – 19 Jan)* Ruby, turquoise, jet, black onyx, clear quartz, black tourmaline

INDEX

PICTURE CREDITS
The publishers would like to thank the following agencies for permission to reproduce their images:
Bruce Coleman Limited: 77, 79, 80bl, 80br, 86b, 87r, 88t, 92bl, 97t, 99t, 100br, 101tr, 120bl, 122, 125
Edimedia: 19l
E.T. Archive: 13r, 14l, 74bl&tr, 76t
Images: The Charles Walker Collection: 18r
Tony Stone Images: 12, 14r, 18l, 20l, 21r, 22, 23r, 29, 39, 47, 75, 80t, 120t
Key: t = top, b = bottom, l = left, r = right

AUTHORS' ACKNOWLEDGEMENTS
Sally Morningstar thanks: Andrew Johnson from the Ayurvedic Trading Company for his invaluable professional guidance; Collette Prideux Brune, aromatherapist; Sarah Duffin at Anness Publishing for her unfailing persistence with a complex subject; and my deepest thanks to the divine will of God – for everything!
    Simon Lilly thanks the following for the loan of crystals: Kay Harrison, Brian Parsons, Sue Lilly, Richard Howard of Arcamia, Bath; Mark O'Leary of The Gem Mine, Exeter; and Mike Davies of Evolution, Exeter.